Praise for J[

"When Jesus viewed the cross, He sp[...]...[...]g us" the joy set before me." He was speaking of the redeemed...we are "His" joy. As her friend, I was given the privilege to walk this path of suffering with Brenda. She never wavered in the hope that her suffering had eternal value and that she would one day look upon all of it with great joy. Her book is a testimony of living life as "His" joy, the difference His presence makes and the belief that God will redeem our suffering as He uses it to impact His kingdom for all eternity."

Donna Ward
Ladies Ministry Leader and Counselor

"Brenda has provided us with a tool born out of her life experiences and walk with the Lord that can help others know what it means to have real 'Joy'."

Dr. Mike Hamlet
Senior Pastor
First Baptist North Spartanburg

"Each of us has the responsibility to share the Gospel through our daily lives. Brenda McGraw has done this fully through genuine expressions of faith, studying and teaching scripture, and personally challenging me to be diligent in my calling in the Body of Christ. She has been a personal mentor and friend to many of the women in our Bible Fellowship Class. When she has been stretched in difficult circumstances, she shines brightly in Christ's love and is evidence that "the joy of the Lord is her strength." This is a wonderful study for all ages and levels of maturity."

Ellen Bunch
Proofreader/Editor
Media Specialist

"In *Joy Beyond*, Brenda challenges readers to not allow their circumstances to rule them, but how to rule over circumstances by focusing on Jesus and looking to Him to provide peace during difficult times. Brenda is uniquely qualified to share the hope of having joy as she has endured many painful and uncertain times in her life. The transparency of her journey is sure to be an inspiration to many and her practical advice will lead others to find joy beyond unpleasant circumstances."

Stacie L. Buck
Author of e-Book, *Transformed, 30 Day Devotional*
President & Founder Diamond Shapers International, LLC
www.diamondshapers.com

"Brenda, I thank God you came into my life as a neighbor and mentor. You will never know how much this Bible study has strengthened my walk with Christ, and changed my life. Everyone should have this book."

Brooke Cooley

"If you want to draw strength in everyday life – read and share this book!"

Glenda Warner

"I have learned to look in the mirror – trying to remove the plank from my own eye."

Stephanie LaValle

"I recommend this book to anyone. My mom wrote it! It is for anyone who finds themselves unhappy or not being positive. There is JOY BEYOND what you are going through."

Melissa Martin

Joy Beyond

Joy Beyond

28 Days to Finding Joy
Beyond the Clutter of Life

Brenda McGraw

For God,
My Father, My Savior, I love You Lord with all of my heart! Thank You for never giving up on me. I pray I will exalt You and bring You glory and honor. Open the doors and I will follow!

For Jeff,
The man who knew God had a plan for me to write before I married him and has supported me through the long hours of writing and editing. I love you. Thanks for loving me the way you do!

For my children, Melissa and Clay,
"I'll love you forever, my baby you'll be." You are my beautiful and precious children. I have always tried to give you stability through the hard times in life. I have tried to live a godly example of Christ in front of you. I pray you will follow your dreams and surrender your hearts and lives to Christ.

Ashley, Matthew and Hannah,
I could never replace your real Mom but I am so thankful God allowed me to be a part of your lives. I know it's not always been easy, but wow have we come a long way! I love you all!

For my grandchildren, Evie and Savannah,
"Nonnie" loves you sooooo much! You light up my world. You bring joy to my heart! I know God has special plans for you and all of my grandchildren!

For Ellen, Dwayne and all my friends,
Thank you for your support, love and friendship. You never gave up on me. I love you all!

Table of Contents

FOREWORD

One day, approximately ten years ago Brenda McGraw walked into my office. She was broken and desperate for her marriage to be salvaged. She was with her husband at the time and by all appearances, they looked like a normal couple.

My name is David Cox and I am a Christian Life Coach who works with couples and individuals. It is my desire to help families stay together and work on ways to repair marriages. It is my passion and purpose to help each individual draw closer to the Lord and live in obedience to God and His commands.

God created marriage to be between one man and one woman. He says in Genesis 2:24, *"Therefore a man shall leave his father and his mother and hold fast to his wife, and they shall become one flesh."* When a marriage fails, there is a tearing of the heart as if it is literally ripped apart. This is what Brenda was experiencing.

Brenda and her husband had been married over twenty years when they first came to me. After sitting down with them I realized that the root cause of the marital problems was immorality due to the sin of her husband. When there is sin in a marriage in the form of immorality of one partner, whether it is adultery, addiction, abuse or any other major sin, you usually have one partner who is willing to do whatever it takes to save the marriage and one partner who may say they are willing, but the stronghold overpowers them. Many times, you have two people, and one is ready to throw in the towel, while the other spouse wants to save the marriage. What I saw in this marriage was Brenda, who loved the Lord and just wanted to get her husband help to overcome his sin and fix their marriage; and I saw her husband who at first said he would do whatever it takes to save the marriage, but was bound to his sin.

After just a few sessions Brenda's husband quit coming to the sessions. His sinful pattern had gotten worse and there were threats made. He abandoned his family. I never saw any resentment or hatred from Brenda towards her spouse. She just wanted him to get

1

"How lovely is your dwelling place,
  O Lord of Heaven's Armies.
I long, yes, I faint with longing
  to enter the courts of the Lord.
With my whole being, body and soul,
  I will shout joyfully to the living God.
Even the sparrow finds a home,
  and the swallow builds her nest and raises her young
at a place near your altar,
  O Lord of Heaven's Armies, my King and my God!
What joy for those who can live in your house,
  always singing your praises. Interlude

What joy for those whose strength comes from the Lord,
  who have set their minds on a pilgrimage to Jerusalem.
When they walk through the Valley of Weeping,
  it will become a place of refreshing springs.
  The autumn rains will clothe it with blessings.
They will continue to grow stronger,
  and each of them will appear before God in Jerusalem.

O Lord God of Heaven's Armies, hear my prayer.
  Listen, O God of Jacob. Interlude

O God, look with favor upon the king, our shield!
  Show favor to the one you have anointed.

A single day in your courts
  is better than a thousand anywhere else!
I would rather be a gatekeeper in the house of my God
  than live the good life in the homes of the wicked.

For the Lord God is our sun and our shield.
  He gives us grace and glory.
The Lord will withhold no good thing
  from those who do what is right.
O Lord of Heaven's Armies,
  what joy for those who trust in you."

Psalm 84 (NLT)

INTRODUCTION

Ten years ago my world as I knew it, fell apart. I was the wife of my high school sweetheart, the mother of two beautiful kids, a homeowner, a successful Insurance agent, and Sunday school teacher. I had survived breast cancer and I should be happy. Why did I not have joy in my heart? How could I go from being all these, yet so empty inside?

My marriage of 23 years ended. I found myself alone with my two young children and I felt broken beyond repair. Day after day I cried and begged God to help me, and my family. My heart was wounded and I grieved the death of my marriage. The pain through the tears had me holding onto the only thing I thought could heal me, God.

I prayed and asked God to heal my heart and my hurts, and to fill me up with more of Him and His joy. Psalm 126 says: *"Our mouths were filled with laughter, our tongues with songs of joy. Then it was said among the nations, 'The LORD has done great things for them.' The LORD has done great things for us, and* **we are filled with joy**. *Restore our fortunes, O LORD, like streams in the Negev.* **Those who sow in tears will reap with songs of joy.** *He who goes out weeping, carrying seed to sow, will return with songs of joy, carrying sheaves with him."*

God took away my pain and filled me to capacity. My cup overflows and my heart sings songs of joy. This doesn't mean that I don't have troubles or problems, it just means I now try to keep my eyes and thoughts on Jesus and His plans. I know He has a purpose for the pain. I know He has plans for His people.

> *"For you make me glad by your deeds, LORD;*
> *I sing for joy at what your hands have done.*
> *How great are your works, LORD,*
> *how profound your thoughts!" Psalm 92:4-5 (NIV)*

> **"I've got joy, joy, joy, joy down in my heart!**
> **Where?**
> **Down in my heart!"**

"I will sing of the LORD's great love forever;
with my mouth I will make your faithfulness known
through all generations.
I will declare that your love stands firm forever,
that you have established your faithfulness in heaven itself."

- Psalm 89:1-2 (NIV)

Week One

Joy Down In My Heart

Day 1   Always...

I was singing one minute and crying the next. I was singing, "I love You, Lord," and crying out to God, begging Him to help me, to change my husband, heal my heart, and to fix my marriage. I was a Christian, but I was a defeated Christian and I was hating the life I was living. I was just going through the motions. I prayed "Take this world from me Lord, I don't need it anymore." I had lived through cancer at the age of 24 and I knew God had a plan and a purpose for me. But life was so devastating and overwhelming. I didn't really care about the future. I was just trying to make it through to the next day, one hour at a time.

Joy was something I didn't have. My face and heart were saddened by all the heartaches and problems. The questions of "why" would dampen my spirit, "Why Lord, is this happening to me?" "Why God, don't you change my husband?" "Why do I get so angry?" " I know You can heal him Jesus. Why don't You?" If You restore my marriage God I know it will bring You glory. Why don't you just heal it Lord?" Why... why... why? My life was cluttered with yuckiness. It was cluttered with the ugly parts that go along with dealing with someone addicted to drugs and the devastation of divorce. I was living "one day at a time."

I remember back in 2002 when times were hard; at church one day, I asked another young lady about joy. She always seemed so happy and she was smiling all the time. You could see the light of Jesus in her. She would tell me, "Jesus is the reason for my joy." I thought to myself, "I know Jesus and I love Him, too, but I don't feel very joyful." I had asked Christ to come into my life five years before. I was going to church, praying, reading my bible, but yet, I still felt it was hard to even smile. I was saddened by the burden I was carrying. I felt no one knew the life I was living at the moment. I was stuck in the life of a wife who was dealing with heartache, pain and helplessness every

Application:

1. Read 1 Thessalonians 5:16-18. Write your name in the blanks.

_____ Always be joyful. _____ Never stop praying. _____ Be thankful in all circumstances, for this is God's will for _____ who belongs to Christ Jesus. 1 Thessalonians 5:16-18 (NLT)

Re-read with your name in the blanks now!

2. What circumstance or problem are you focused on today?

_____

_____

_____

3. What are some ways you can pray without ceasing?

_____

_____

_____

Pray the following prayer:

Dear Father,

I want to be thankful for (your circumstance)

_____

_____.

As crazy as it sounds, Lord help me to be thankful. I know You are with me. I am asking for joy right now, today, as I face this. I believe You are in control and You love me.
In Jesus name, Amen.

Always be joyful and thankful, by praying always!

Breathe new life into your mind. Renew your mind!

> *"Do not conform to the pattern of this world, but be transformed by the renewing of your mind. Then you will be able to test and approve what God's will is—his good, pleasing and perfect will." Romans 12:2 (NIV)*

God wants our thoughts to be focused on Him first and foremost each and every day. However, He knows we will think of other things as well. He wants us to bring those other things to Him and put in to practice handing them to Him daily. As a result of being obedient to this practice, He promises His peace will be with us!

> *"We are destroying speculations and every lofty thing raised up against the knowledge of God, and we are taking every thought captive to the obedience of Christ." 2 Corinthians 10:5 (NASB)*

So, how do we take every thought captive to the obedience of Christ?

We can't always help what thought goes into our mind. Sometimes thoughts come out of nowhere. Before we know it, we are judging someone or thinking the worst. We may suddenly start worrying about something because of a circumstance. We have to be very careful to guard our minds against negative thoughts. We do, however, have control over what stays in our mind and how long it stays there. We need to take the thought captive, measure it against the Word of God, and if it doesn't align with the will or attributes of God, we need to destroy it immediately, before it takes root and affects our action.

I have said many times, "Away from me Satan, I am a child of God." Satan has to flee. Take your thought or worry and turn it into prayer. You can do it. It may take a little practice, but as you progress in your walk with the Lord you will find it easier and easier as time goes on. Practice may not make perfect, but practice makes perfect sense!

4. Ask God to help you fix your thoughts on what is true, honorable, right, pure, lovely, admirable, excellent and praiseworthy.

5. Write your name in the blanks and then read it back aloud and start practicing God's principles to change your thought pattern.

"_____ , do not conform to the pattern of this world, but be transformed by the renewing of _____'s mind. Then _____ will be able to test and approve what God's will is— His good, pleasing and perfect will." "_____ is destroying speculations and every lofty thing raised up against the knowledge of God, and _____ is taking every thought captive to the obedience of Christ."

Write a prayer to God asking Him to forgive you for any thoughts, which may not be pleasing to Him. Ask Him to help you focus your thoughts on Him and to bring peace into your life.

_____

_____

_____

_____

_____

"And now, dear brothers and sisters, one final thing. Fix your thoughts on what is true, and honorable, and right, and pure, and lovely, and admirable. Think about things that are excellent and worthy of praise. Keep putting into practice all you learned and received from me—everything you heard from me and saw me doing. Then the God of peace will be with you."
Philippians 4:8, 9 (NLT)

Day 3   To Do or Not To Do!

To gain joy, we have to give it away!

Are you giving joy away or are you possibly stealing it from others? Ask God to help you be more gentle and kind to those you meet today. Ask Him to help you extend more grace to others. Everybody is busy. Sometimes we get stuck thinking only about what's on our personal agenda. I find when I try to bless someone else, or help them with a problem they are currently facing, my problems don't seem to distract me or upset me quite as much. We can even stop and pray with someone else and it seems to lighten not only their load, but our own. In Acts 20:35, Jesus taught us it is more blessed to give than receive.

To-Do or Not-To-Do, that is the question.

I love having a "To Do" list. It's very satisfying when I can mark things off and I move on to the next thing. It gives me a sense of accomplishment. Occasionally I will write something on my list I need to do for someone else. If you don't currently make "To-Do" lists, I suggest you try making one and actually writing on your list, "Send a card to someone from Bible Fellowship class who is hurting right now." Do we write on our "To Do" list, "Take food to the friend who just had surgery"? Try writing on your list, "Be kind to my kids today by putting a love note in their book bag." We shouldn't have to be reminded to pray with or for a friend who has a struggling marriage or worries about her prodigal child, but put it on your list to ensure you remember.

Whether or not we write things down on our "To Do" list, we do need to practice doing them. I find when I don't write things down I tend to forget to do some things. It holds me accountable to get things done.

mind governed by the flesh is death, but the mind governed by the Spirit is life and peace. The mind governed by the flesh is hostile to God; it does not submit to God's law, nor can it do so. Those who are in the realm of the flesh cannot please God."
Romans 8:5-8 (NASB)

Scripture says:

"Give, and it will be given to you. A good measure, pressed down, shaken together and running over, will be poured into your lap. For with the measure you use, it will be measured to you." Luke 6:38 (NIV)

When we give of ourselves to others, it will come back to us.

The more we give and bless others, the more we will receive and be blessed. What happens when you give a hug to somebody? Most of the time you are getting a hug in return. My dad used to say "you need seven hugs a day." We all need to start hugging more. I am sure there are people who may not receive seven hugs in a week. Hug a friend! Hug your child! Hug your mom! Hug your spouse! People need hugs! You will be blessed in return!

When was the last time you shook someone's hand? You say "hello" or "goodbye" to an acquaintance or say hello to someone you are meeting and you offer your hand for a handshake. What do they do in return? They offer their hand back to you and shake your hand. When you give, it comes back to you. It's the same with giving a blessing to someone. When you offer a blessing or a gift of assistance to someone, the blessing comes 'right back at ya' in return! Try it. Be a blessing to someone!

Do your kids see your kindness or are you always telling them "NO"?

We can start by showing our kids grace when they mess up or when you have asked them for the 100th time to pick up their shoes or clean up their room. A good way to discover if we are gentle and kind is to ask our family. I am sure they will let us know.

Dear Father,

I lift my friends up to You today and pray You will give them the strength to do the things they have listed above. Help them find peace and depend on You today to get these things accomplished, including the acts of kindness. I pray a special blessing on their lives. Please help them with the daily activities, which sometimes are overwhelming. Show them the joy You have for them today Lord!
In Jesus name, I pray. Amen.

> *"Let your gentleness be evident to all. The Lord is near."*
> *Philippians 4:5 (NIV)*

To gain joy, we have to give it away!

Circumstances will always get better. Look through rose colored glasses. There is something good in every situation.

Jesus was a positive man.

He walked in the ways of the fruit of the Spirit. He lived and taught to love one another. He believed and taught *"with God all things are possible."* He said *"ask and it shall be given."* More than 2000 years ago in Luke 8:50, He said, *"Don't be afraid. Just believe."* He believed God is the source of all good things. We are to follow the example of Christ. We are to have the attitude of Christ. Jesus didn't walk around grumbling or complaining when something wasn't going His way. He believed God had a purpose for the bad as well as the good.

In 1 Thessalonians 5:21-22 it says, "...*Hold on to what is good. Stay away from every kind of evil.*" (NLT)

One form of evil is negativism, which is an attitude of being pessimistic or negative. It is ineffective to deal with stress and wrong-doings with negativity. When we are negative we feel bad; we start complaining and blaming others. This turns into a tool to be used by Satan to cause strife and discord. The only way to deal with negativity is overcome evil with good. We can do this only through God's guidance. It is much better to live as Jesus did, with a positive attitude. When we get a bad attitude or have a critical or negative spirit within us, we are allowing our flesh to win. This is not in accordance with God's will and plan for us. I rest assured that I can say, we have all done it. Something upsets us, we get mad and we start complaining. The best way to handle this, is by working on renewing our mind. We can find a scripture verse, listen to an upbeat song, and say a prayer. We can look for the good in all things. The good will always outweigh the negative, if we will look at it though God's eyes.

Application:

1. So, which are you? Negative or positive?

_____

Day 5   His Unfailing Love

Do you believe that God can truly satisfy you? Do you let Him? Ask God to satisfy you with His unfailing love.

Unfailing, really?

We live in a world full of pain and evil. A world where people let us down and we experience failure and disappointment. A world where at times we cause pain and disappointment for others. It's hard for us to really understand the words "unfailing love." Unfailing means "without error or fault," to be "reliable or constant." In Psalm 90:14 the Bible says, *"Satisfy us each morning with your unfailing love, so we may sing for joy to the end of our lives."* We may let God and others down daily, but God's love is unfailing. It's reliable and constant. He will never let you down!

I have to admit there have been times in my life when I doubted God's unfailing love for me. I thought He wasn't answering my prayers the way they should be answered, or should I say, the way I wanted them answered. It wasn't God who failed me; it was me who failed God. I have been way over my head in debt in the past. I couldn't understand why God just wouldn't send me a big check to get me out of the trouble I'd gotten myself into. So I doubted God's love for me. God is not our "genie in a bottle," whom we only call on in times of trouble or times of need. We cannot have the attitude that He is just going to magically appear and poof...our problems are solved.

God is God. He is the Great I AM!

He may allow us to suffer and go through hard times, to teach us a lesson or mold us into His image. Most of the time He wants to teach

Dear Lord,

"But <u>Brenda</u> trusts in Your unfailing love. <u>Brenda</u> will rejoice because You have rescued <u>Brenda</u>." Thank You Lord, for rescuing <u>Brenda</u> and helping <u>Brenda</u> always to trust Your plans.

In Jesus Name!

Amen.

> *"My heart is confident in you, O God; my heart is confident. No wonder I can sing your praises! For your unfailing love is as high as the heavens. Your faithfulness reaches to the clouds." Psalm 57:7, 10 (NLT)*

> *"O God, you are my God; I earnestly search for you. My soul thirsts for you; my whole body longs for you in this parched and weary land where there is no water. Your unfailing love is better than life itself; how I praise you! I will praise you as long as I live, lifting up my hands to you in prayer. You satisfy me more than the richest feast. I will praise you with songs of joy." Psalm 63:1, 3-5 (NLT)*

> *"Let your unfailing love surround us, Lord, for our hope is in you alone." Psalm 33:22 (NLT)*

> *"For he satisfies the thirsty and fills the hungry with good things." Psalm 107:9 (NLT)*

> *"When you open your hand, you satisfy the hunger and thirst of every living thing. The Lord is righteous in everything he does; he is filled with kindness. He grants the desires of those who fear him; he hears their cries for help and rescues them." Psalm 145:16, 17, 19 (NLT)*

I have given you space on the next page to write your prayer with the scripture you have chosen.

Day 6   *God Use Me*

Ask God if you are seeing the world from His perspective. Be prepared for the answer, because in most cases His answer is clearly no. Why are we such unstable people? One minute we are on "fire for God" and the next minute we have one foot in the world. Our world!

What does your world look like? Is God pleased with it?

Maybe you have a wonderful family and you get up every day and do the same happy routine. You get the kids ready for school, you get yourself ready for work and you are out the door. Oops...no time for God; but you say, "I will pray on the way to work." But oh no, you forgot to pray. Then you get to work and enter the hustle and bustle of the day. Before you know it, it's time to go home. You think to yourself, "We have baseball tonight...again, so I've got to hurry." You stop by the store and pick up something for dinner. Then you hurry home to cook it, help your children with their homework, and off to the game. It is late when you get home and you get the kids in the bath. You hurry, you stress, and argue with the kids. You barely have time to speak to your spouse. You finally get the kids in the bed! Whew! Ah man, you remember, "I can't forget I have that mound of laundry to do and dishes in the sink that have to be done." By the end of the day, you're exhausted and you go to bed just so you can get up early in the morning and do the same thing over again. Oops, no time for God again. You say to yourself and God, "I will pray when I lie down." As you are praying...well you know what happens; you fall asleep.

This is our own little world. Can you tell I have been there? This may or may not be where you are in your life right now. It's all important stuff. I realized back in those days of small kids and crazy schedules that something needed to change if I was going to make

4. _____

5. _____

6. _____

God says it should be:

1.   God
2.   Spouse
3.   Children & Family
4.   Ministry
5.   Job
6.   Everything else

How are you doing with your priorities? Ask God to help you get your priorities in the proper order according to His will.

> *"Do not waver, for a person with divided loyalty is as unsettled as a wave of the sea that is blown and tossed by the wind. Their loyalty is divided between God and the world, and they are unstable in everything they do." James 1:5, 6, 8 (NLT)*

4. Write a prayer and ask God to help you get your priorities in the right order. Ask Him to help you see the world the way He does and give you opportunities today to serve others.

_____

_____

_____

_____

_____

Wishy-washy faith leaves a life a little unsafe.

"Many, LORD, are asking, "Who will bring us prosperity?"
Let the light of your face shine on us.
Fill my heart with joy
when their grain and new wine abound."
Psalm 4:7 (NLT)

Do you want to sing "I've got the joy, joy, joy, joy down in my heart"?

Sure we do! We want our hearts to smile and rejoice and we can do that when we can say "I've been with Jesus today." Take your eyes off whatever is stealing your joy today and look at Jesus. He has joy for you! Just spend some time with Him and ask Him!!

"Though you have not seen him, you love him; and even though you do not see him now, you believe in him and are filled with an inexpressible and glorious joy." 1 Peter 1:8 (NIV)

I started the Introduction of this book with the chorus of the song below. As I mentioned, I went through a stretch of my life where I felt joyless and I could not truthfully sing this song. I was so weighed down by my circumstances. When people told me they could see Jesus in me, it was only through His amazing grace! Grace would bring a smile to my face when I didn't feel like smiling. Grace would comfort me when I just wanted to cry. This is the grace that is given by God. Joy comes from Jesus. Smile, people need to see the joy in your heart. Bear your fruit for Jesus, the joy Giver!

I've Got the Joy In My Heart, by George Willis Cooke

I've got the joy, joy, joy, joy down in my heart
Where?
Down in my heart!
Where?
Down in my heart!
I've got the joy, joy, joy, joy down in my heart
Down in my heart to stay

_____

_____

_____

_____

_____

4. Write a prayer to God thanking the Lord for your salvation. Ask Him to help you find the true joy that only He can give you.

_____

_____

_____

_____

_____

_____

If you don't already know and have a relationship with Christ, I have enclosed the steps to finding salvation through Jesus.

Steps to Salvation:

To know God and be ready for heaven, follow these steps:

A. Admit you are a sinner.

"There is no one righteous, not even one … for all have sinned and fall short of the glory of God."
Romans 3:10, 23 (NIV) (See Romans 5:8; 6:23)

Ask God's forgiveness.

"Everyone who calls on the name of the Lord will be saved."
Romans 10:13 (NIV)

B. Believe in Jesus.

(Put your trust in Him) as your only hope of salvation.
"For God so loved the world that he gave his one and only Son, that whoever believes in him shall not perish but have eternal life." John 3:16 (NIV) (See John 14:6)

Become a child of God by receiving Christ.

redeemed you for a price! The price was His death on the cross. May God bless you!

If you prayed to receive Christ into your life, please let me know by contacting me through my website at **www.askgodtoday.com**, so that I can rejoice with you and help you get started with your walk with Christ!

The joy of salvation is revealed through God's footprints in the sand, and His handprints on your heart.

Week Two

The God of Hope

Day 8   *God's Face Shines Upon You!*

> *"May God be gracious to us and bless us and make his face shine on us..." Psalm 67:1 (NIV)*

Welcome to Week Two. I hope you enjoyed the first week and have found some meaningful scripture to apply to your life. Today, we will be focusing on the favor of God. Do you need God's favor? The favor of God is when He shines His face upon you and is gracious to you. To "favor" means to give special regard to and show extra kindness to someone. God can and will show favor to you. He gives you grace and peace in the midst of your circumstances. Receiving favor sometimes means that we are treated better than we even expect. Naturally, we are filled with joy when we have been shown God's favor. Ask God to extend His favor to you in whatever circumstance you are currently facing.

Recently, someone I love was shown favor by God. He lives a life that in all appearances is very pleasing to the Lord. He was going through a difficult time and by prayer and committing the situation to God, his prayers were answered and God gave him peace in the midst of the circumstance. The Lord, our Father, will do that for you as well. He loves you and wants to show you His favor and blessings. He delights in seeing His people find joy and happiness.

So, how can WE win favor in God's sight and man's?

It is not required by God that we do anything to gain favor in His eyes. He gives because He loves us! He just plain loves us! He shows His grace to us because He loves us. He loves you and He loves me! However, He tells us in His Word our love and faithfulness to Him will win favor in His eyes and in the eyes of man.

to those who please Him. I want God to be pleased with me. Don't you?

Get into God's Word and God's Word will get into you!

> *"May the Lord bless you and protect you. May the Lord smile on you and be gracious to you. May the Lord show you His favor and give you His peace." Numbers 6:24-26 (NLT)*

Application:

1. What is one prayer request you have been praying where you need God to show you His favor and kindness?

   _____

   _____

   _____

2. Write your name in the blanks of the scripture listed below and then re-read:

   "May the Lord bless _____ and protect _____.
   May the Lord smile on _____ and be gracious to
   _____. May the Lord show _____ His favor and
   give _____ His peace."

3. If you don't have a time set aside everyday for "quiet time" with the Lord, consider making a commitment to the Lord, giving Him 15 to 30 minutes of your day. Write a prayer below to make this commitment to the Lord. Ask God to bless you and show you favor. He will help you take one day at a time, starting today, by increasing this special time with Him.

   _____

   _____

   _____

   _____

Day 9   Zap the Fear

Fear can easily rob us of our joy.

When you are walking in fear, the enemy, Satan, uses this to blind you. It is his plan to keep you from trusting the Lord, whatever your circumstances might be right now. We can ask God to help us overcome our fear of things to come. Did you know God wants you to have the victory in this world too? He knows that we are confronted with daily struggles and face battles that we can't fight alone.

Do you believe that since God is for you, no one can be against you? Romans 8:31 states, *"If God is for us, who can ever be against us?"* NO ONE! It goes on to say, when you have been chosen to be His own, then no one can be against you. God has given us right standing with Himself. Christ Jesus died for us, He was raised for us and He is pleading for us!!

This doesn't necessarily mean that everything is going to always work out the way we think it should. We live in a sinful, fallen world. God is working all things together for the good of those who love Him.

Many times **we need God's favor when dealing with people.** When we are going through a situation, where we don't know what to say or do, He is there. When we feel like we have done what is right, and we don't know of anything we did wrong; God will be there with us helping us overcome! He will go before us on our behalf. He will help us defeat the struggles and battles that we face daily. He's got my back and He's got your back too! He is not going to leave us.

Sometimes we can step into a situation in life where someone is just hard to deal with, due to their bitterness, and you become the target.

As a mature believer in Christ, we need to keep seeking God, praying, and living a life that pleases Him. Let God handle your difficulties and circumstances for you. We cannot change other people. We can only trust and release it to the One who can! If God is for you, then trust that He has this under control for you! Also, know there is always a purpose for whatever God allows us to go through.

> "What shall we say about such wonderful things as these? If God is for us, who can ever be against us? Since he did not spare even his own Son but gave Him up for us all, won't He also give us everything else? Who dares accuse us whom God has chosen for His own? No one—for God himself has given us right standing with himself. Who then will condemn us? No one—for Christ Jesus died for us and was raised to life for us, and He is sitting in the place of honor at God's right hand, pleading for us. Can anything ever separate us from Christ's love? Does it mean He no longer loves us if we have trouble or calamity, or are persecuted, or hungry, or destitute, or in danger, or threatened with death? No, despite all these things, overwhelming victory is ours through Christ, who loved us."
> Romans 8:31-35, 37 (NLT)

Application:

1. What are you personally walking through right now, that you foresee a fearful outcome? Don't doubt the power of Christ and dread the outcome; instead, write a prayer asking for God's favor.

_____

_____

_____

_____

_____

2. Write a prayer to God and ask Him the following:

   a) Ask God to take away the fear and the jitters you are facing.

spirit of fear, but of power and of love and of a sound mind." 2 Timothy 1:7 (KJV)

I would ask for wisdom, discernment, and for God to be with me, and never leave me. I would cry out to Jesus and ask Him to help me. I would pray asking the Lord to take away my fear and help me trust him. I studied scripture day after day, stayed in Bible studies, and surrounded myself with godly people. God carried me through. He took away the trembling at night. **He took away the fear and that's when I realized and found out what it really means to walk by faith and not fear.**

Faith not fear, joy not jitters.

say a prayer asking for the person's need to be met, but that's not the only time we should be praying. We tend to mutter a quick little 15-second prayer at times, which is praying continuously like God instructs. However, as great as that is, and it is certainly better than not praying at all, it just isn't all that the Lord has for us.

God wants a close and personal relationship with us.

He wants to spend time with us so He can guide us to trust Him. He wants to show us His faithfulness. Not to throw a guilt trip on us, but chances are we spend a whole lot more time scrolling through Facebook all day or socializing, than investing time conversing with the Creator and Savior of the world.

I grew up believing in God and would even pray to God. **I thought I was a Christian but later realized I didn't know Jesus.** Just praying to God without a personal relationship with Jesus isn't enough. He wants to know us. He wants to spend time with us. He desires to hear the prayer of surrender. When I finally realized I didn't really know Jesus, I only knew of Him and I prayed asking God to show me who Jesus is, that is when my life went from self prayers to surrendered prayers.

This Scripture in James says, *"The earnest **prayer** of a righteous person has great power and produces wonderful results."* We will never be righteous unless we **strive** for righteousness and even then, we fall short. We have to strive for full surrender. That's when it becomes "not about me, but all about Him." Strive means "to make strenuous efforts toward any goal, to strive for success, to exert oneself vigorously; try hard." Do we strive for righteousness? Only you and God really know. He is the One we are striving to know and be more like. It's His purpose for us to bring Him glory and to be transformed into the image of Christ. We can't do it alone. It's a daily surrender. A daily laying down of our own selfish fleshly ways and picking up the cross of Christ.

When we strive to pray surrendered prayers instead of selfish prayers, our prayers produce power and wonderful results through the cross of Christ.

He has drawn me closer to Himself every day since I received the dreaded news of cancer. In August 1995 when my son was seven months old, I laid down my old life and picked up the new life that Jesus gave me. This was the beginning of surrendering my ways and actions to Him! My life changed tremendously!

Faith Brings Joy

> *"Therefore, since we have been made right in God's sight by faith, we have peace with God because of what Jesus Christ our Lord has done for us. Because of our faith, Christ has brought us into this place of undeserved privilege where we now stand, and we confidently and joyfully look forward to sharing God's glory. We can rejoice, too, when we run into problems and trials, for we know that they help us develop endurance. And endurance develops strength of character, and character strengthens our confident hope of salvation. **And this hope will not lead to disappointment.** For we know how dearly God loves us, because he has given us the Holy Spirit to fill our hearts with his love." Romans 5:1-5 (NLT)*

How often do you wake up and thank God for giving you another day to live?

He chose me first, and eventually I chose to surrender my life to Him! My life is His! I don't know what tomorrow will bring, none of us do! We may be here today and gone tomorrow.

How will you choose to live your daily agenda, the day God has given you? What about your future and your dreams, would they be pleasing to God? What does God want you to do with your life? He has a plan for you that is dependent on a surrendered life. Once we belong to Him, He will reveal His purpose to us for our life. I am thankful that God has given me each morning since those days in 1986 to LIVE LIFE! I want to live it well! What about you?

I look back now 27 years ago, see the plan a little better, and understand why God allowed cancer in my life at such a young age. It was my bottom, the end of my old life and the birth of a new one!

Application:

1. Write a prayer and ask God what He wants you to do with your life?

_____

_____

_____

_____

_____

_____

_____

Sometimes we think we have it all figured but we don't even have a clue. We think, our agenda, our plan, our future, our kids, our house, our car. OURS, really? None of it belongs to us. God allows us to manage them, but ultimately they ALL belong to Him!

2. What sin are you hanging on to from your old life that you need to surrender to God?

_____

_____

3. Ask God to help you release it to Him, so you can become the "new person" He wants you to be.

4. What is the most recent "something" in your life that has upset you, or rocked your world?

_____

_____

_____

_____

How did you handle it? Anger ____ Tears ____ Fear ____ Faith____

Day 12   He is Faithful!

His righteous right hand holds me forever!

We can ask God to uphold us with His righteous right hand. To uphold means to rise up, to support, and to prevent from falling or sinking. What do you need God to uphold for you today? On the day that I wrote this, I had an ultrasound for a follow up mammogram. It has been 27 years ago today that I had breast cancer and had a mastectomy. Every year for the last 26 years when I went for my yearly mammogram, they always seemed to find something they needed to evaluate further. So far, for all those years the results had been benign.

I know it is the power of God upholding me, and the power of all the prayers of my family and friends! I am so grateful for those who have prayed for me over these years. So on this day, I once again was asking for prayer. My prayer was that God would be gracious to me, and once again, this would be nothing of concern.

My God is faithful, and He gave me a precious verse to share. If we will take time out of our busy days, sit, listen and look into His Word and pray, He will speak into our heart and give us exactly what we need for the day! So again, I ask, what do you need God to uphold for you today? HE IS GOD!

> *"So do not fear, for I am with you; do not be dismayed, for I am your God. I will strengthen you and help you; I will uphold you with my righteous right hand." Isaiah 41:10 (NIV)*

God doesn't want us to walk in daily fear of the unknown. Don't lose courage and dread the outcome. He tells us He will give His

_____

_____

_____

4. Today, please look up the following Scriptures in your Bible or on your phone or iPad: Isaiah 41: 8-10. Let's break these verses down a little.

God had been talking to all nations, telling them of the coming judgment because of their denial of who He is. However, in verse 8, God speaks specifically to His chosen nation, Israel, comforting them by telling them they have been chosen. God continues to speak to His chosen followers to this day; the chosen are you and I who have made a conscious decision to follow Christ.

What does God tell Israel and us in verse 9? Fill in your name:

_"I took _____ from the ends of the Earth, from its farthest corners I called _____. I said, '_____ you are my servant; I have chosen _____ and have not rejected _____.'"_

God has more to tell us in verse 10. Fill in the blanks with your name.

_"So do not fear, for I am with _____; do not be dismayed, for I am _____'s God. I will strengthen _____ and help _____; I will uphold _____ with my righteous right hand." Isaiah 41:10 (NIV)_

God is not going to leave you or reject you.

He wants you to know Him, trust Him and surrender your life fully to Him. He has chosen you. Do you believe that? ☺

Day 13   *Is God Your Everything?*

Do you need more joy today?

We can ask God to be our everything!

Here is a prayer I wrote in my journal several months ago. I wanted to share it with you because it clearly states how God CAN BE our everything. What does it mean to make God your everything? What does it mean to make God priority in your life?

Dear Father, my Lord, my Jesus!

You are my God, my Savior, and my Redeemer! You are my Counselor, my Comforter, my Protector and my Provider! God you are my Everything! You are my King who brings peace, joy and love to my life! You fill me up daily! I need you! I desire you! I want to always live my life for You! You pick me up and You forgive me when I fall! You comfort me when I am sad! You heal me when I am sick! You lead me, you guide me and You are a lamp unto my feet! You correct me when I stray and turn me around to go the other way! You are my Forever! You created me, you molded me and YOU LOVE ME! You will never leave me, nor forsake me! You have saved me from destruction and eternal separation and I am Yours! For all of this and so much more I am forever grateful to the One who calls me His daughter!

I love you!

In Jesus name, I pray.

Amen.

According to Matthew 6:33 quoted above, what are we supposed to seek first? It says, *"seek first His kingdom and His righteousness."* We talked about priorities back in Day 6. God gives us a promise in verse 33 here. He tells us if we seek Him and His kingdom and righteousness first, then "all these things" will be provided as well. Therefore, what are "all these things"? **What is that promise "there for?"** It is there for you and me to realize God has a plan for us and will provide for all our needs, but we have to do our part. Our part is to SEEK. To seek is to look for, to earnestly search for (someone or something), to ask for help, or advice. It means to try to discover.

To seek His kingdom and righteousness first, we are to look and search for God, to discover who He is and ask for His help, FIRST!

Now, I am not forgetting the reality of how busy we are. We have to work, raise our children and love our spouse and others. These are all very important and take a lot of our time. God knows better than I do how much time is needed to prepare meals, clean up, take kids to school, go to programs, give baths, be a good wife or husband, adult child, friend, or employee, etc. **He wants us to serve others, but seek HIM first!**

He promises us in His Word; if we seek Him first, He will help us with all these other things. He will help us be a better spouse, a better mom or dad. He will show us how to be a better employee or boss. He will provide for "all these things." **If these things are important to us, they are important to God**.

Application:

Do Not Worry

1. Read Matthew 6:25-34

> *"Therefore I tell you, do not worry about your life, what you will eat or drink; or about your body, what you will wear. Is not life more than food, and the body more than clothes? Look at the birds of the air; they do not sow or reap or store away in barns, and yet your heavenly Father feeds them. Are you not much*

5. Write a prayer confessing to God the things you have put before Him. He already knows. He will not judge you. He is a God of grace and love and He is waiting patiently for you to come closer to Him. He wants to fill you with His joy! Ask Him:

_____

_____

_____

_____

_____

"My flesh and my heart may fail, but God is the strength of my heart and my portion forever." Psalm 73:26 (NIV)

Everything you need, you will have, when God becomes everything you need!

To whom do you cry for help? From where does your help come?

When we are in trouble, we tend to go to our spouse, parents or friends first. Then, when that doesn't seem to help us out of the problem, we pray and ask God to help.

We should always go to God first. If He leads us to someone for help, that's fine. The bottom line is we need to put our trust in the Savior of the World before people.

Whom do you trust?

If we want to find joy, we need to be spending time with the One who is trustworthy and gives joy. We too easily trust just anybody. I see this mostly in kids. They will jump right into friendships without knowing anything about the person. Unfortunately, we live in a world where people can be evil and can hurt others.

When you place your trust in Christ and surrender your life to Him, He will give you wisdom to choose your friends wisely. He will give you the desire to live a righteous life and to do what is right.

Surrender, have we talked about surrender? What does it looks like to have a surrendered life? **A life fully surrendered to God is a life fully abandoned from self.**

How do we abandon self and surrender to God? We completely leave the ways of self-admiration, self-conceit, self-exaltation, self-importance, and self-love. We give up the control of our life to God, yielding to His ways and guidance. Meaning we lay down what we want and pick up what God wants. We don't just do this today, but every day for the rest of our life.

We can't do this on our own; it's only through the grace of God. It's in our nature to naturally want to make ourselves look good. God wants it to become our nature to exalt Him and make Him look good. Now, don't get me wrong. He doesn't need us to do this. He is God! He allows us to get to know Him, and who He is through Jesus Christ and then He will use us to glorify His name. Many times He allows us to go

4. I want you to end this week by finding some uplifting, happy, fun praise music, and turn it up loud in your home or car and sing to Jesus! Praising Him and worshipping Him for your life!!

Here are few song suggestions, but you can choose others:

Hold On, by Jamie Grace
Stronger, by Mandisa
Good Morning, by Mandisa
Get Back Up, by Toby Mac
So Long Self, by Mercy Me
Overcomer, by Mandisa

5. Tomorrow, write down your experience. How did the songs make you feel? Did you sing? Did you feel a moment of joy?

_____

_____

_____

_____

_____

_____

This is the end of our second week together. I am praying for you. I am praying God inspires you to live a life of joy and peace. I pray He draws you close to Him and gives you a hunger and desire for more of Him! He is the Joy Giver! Quoting from the songs listed, "Hold On" just a little bit longer, these hard times will make you "Stronger." "So Long Self," I am an "Overcomer" and in the morning, it's going to be a "Good Morning" and I will "Get Back Up" again!

When you lift your heart in praise, you lift your hands in prayer!

Week Three
Don't Give Up

Day 15   Stand Astonished

It's already the third week. Thank you for sticking with me. I am excited to announce that this is the first book I have written and I thank you for spending your time with me. My purpose is to bring God glory through the words of these pages and to let you know that even when this life gets overwhelming to us, God is not overwhelmed. I am praying for you as you continue to read and study God's Word with me. I pray that our sweet precious Lord will draw your heart close to His heart!

Paul explained his purpose in Colossians 2:2-3. This should be our purpose as well. *"My purpose is that they may be encouraged in heart and united in love, so that they may have the full riches of complete understanding, in order that they may know the mystery of God, namely Christ, in whom are hidden all the treasures of wisdom and knowledge." (NIV)*

Ask God to lead the way.

Today, as I spent time reading and praying in my quiet time with the Lord, I read Isaiah 30:21. It reminded me that most of the time we don't know what the next step is or where God is leading. Do you know where He is leading you? Aren't there times when we all wish we could know what the next ten years of our life will look like?

> *"Whether you turn to the right or to the left, your ears will hear a voice behind you, saying, 'This is the way; walk in it'."*
> *Isaiah 30:21 (NIV)*

Is Jesus leading the way in your life?

In Mark 10:32a it says, *"They were on their way up to Jerusalem,*

Sometimes, we become fearful of the unknown or what lies before us. It was especially hard after going through a divorce. I didn't know what my life was going to be like. I had been married for 23 years. That was all of my adult life. I had married at 19 and found myself single, scared and all alone with two children.

It was then that I realized that God was not only my Father, but could be my husband, too. I had never heard that before.

> *"For your Maker is your husband--the LORD Almighty is his name--the Holy One of Israel is your Redeemer; he is called the God of all the earth." Isaiah 54:5 (NIV)*

I became totally dependent on the Lord. I didn't have anybody else who I could depend on. God, the Father, became my husband! This is when He became my EVERYTHING! When I didn't know what to do, I would spend time with Him, my Father and my Husband. He filled me up when I was empty. He embraced me with His touch and His warmth when I was lonely. He pointed me in the direction I was to go, while holding my hand and walking beside me, like a godly husband would do. **He was carrying me over the threshold, through the doors of life.** I prayed and asked God to help me take one day at a time. I asked Him to give me my daily bread for "today." I would pray and ask God to help me not to make mistakes. He is faithful! All we have to do is our part. We need to trust, seek, and obey!

If you are going through a fearful time, pray and ask the Lord to give you His courage! It may be a time of suffering, which the Lord is allowing you to go through, just so He can lead, comfort, and draw you close to His precious heart of love. He wants to embrace you, dry your tears, and bring joy back into your heart. If someone has abandoned you and you are walking in the fear of the unknown, the Lord will never leave you. He will calm the fears and storms.

Here are three different versions of this beautiful verse showing God comforts us and brings joy, hope, and cheer to our souls!

> *"I cried out, "I am slipping!"*
> *but your unfailing love, O LORD, supported me.*

I love the song by Chris Tomlin, called "Whom Shall I Fear." The song tells us there is no need to fear because we know who goes before us, and who stands behind us. It's the God of angel armies who is always by our side.

This is so true for a follower of Jesus. God does go before us and is leading the way and He is also standing behind us, ready to catch us when we fall. He is ALWAYS by our side! Even when we are afraid of what the next step is, or an unknown future, God is there leading us and walking through it with us!

When we decide in our own mind, what we hope will happen, and try to plan it all out, we need to ask, "Is this God's plan for me?" Don't let yourself get ahead of God. Let Him lead you and watch in astonishment all the wonders and glories He has prepared for you!

> "The Lord is my light and my salvation—whom shall I fear? The Lord is the stronghold of my life—of whom shall I be afraid?" Psalm 27:1 (NIV)

> "The Lord himself goes before you and will be with you; he will never leave you nor forsake you. Do not be afraid; do not be discouraged." Deuteronomy 31:8 (NIV)

Application:

1. What do you need God's guidance in today?

_____

_____

_____

_____

_____

2. Fill in your name in the following scripture:

> "The Lord himself goes before _____ and will be with

Day 16   The Brighter Side

Cast your eyes on the brighter side of life.

Have you ever woken up and wanted to just turn over and not get out of the bed? Sure, I bet we all have from time to time. I went through a recent time of not sleeping well at night. I would wake up and stay awake one to two hours tossing and turning. My mind would race with all kinds of thoughts, and I would easily get distracted from the Lord. It's those times in the middle of the night I try to turn my worries to prayer.

When you can't sleep, pray instead of worry. Count your blessings instead of sheep.

During a restless night of sleep, we have a choice. We can let the lack of sleep cause us to be grouchy, mean and ugly to the ones we love OR we can look on the bright side!!

What does the bright side look like?

It's sunshine after the rain, joy through the pain, and happiness to gain. Look on the bright side; behold the beauty all around you. Notice the flowers blooming and the trees changing, whether winter, spring, summer, or fall. There is always beauty around us. Enjoy an evening outdoors with your family, and evening walks. On those nights you sleep well, try rising a little earlier and checkout the beautiful sunrise in the mornings. Enjoy the splendor of the sunset glowing over the lakes and ocean. God has the power to turn the blue sky into a ray of colors for our eyes to gaze upon, reflecting the glorious awe-inspiring beauty. This beauty reflects the most amazing artist of the entire universe, the Majesty of the Lord Almighty! To God be the glory! We do not want to miss the magnificence of what He can create

God revealed this verse to me many years ago, not long after I first believed and committed my life to Him. I was so excited when I found this verse; it was as if I were the only one in the whole world who had ever found it. I held on to every word, every promise God had for me through the words of this verse. I highlighted, wrote it in my journal and prayed, thanking God for His plans for me. Later, I realized it was the life verse for many people.

God will speak to you if you let Him. He has great plans for you. He says all we have to do is seek Him with all of our heart. I took those words of God and put them in action. I started seeking and He started giving me the greatest hope I had ever experienced. My future is in His hands. Your future is in His hands.

> "Now to him who is able to do immeasurably more than all we ask or imagine, according to his power that is at work within us…" Ephesians 3:20

So, we have to get out of our pity parties and start making a difference. Go meet your neighbors! Take a mission trip! Lead a Bible study or teach a class. Write a book!

Life is full of opportunities. The world is beautiful! Make the best of every day and every opportunity!

Joy is a choice.

You can look for the blessing in the midst of the messes of life and choose joy or you can sit around discouraged and without hope. My God tells me, *"Do not grieve, for the joy of the Lord is your strength."*

The choice is yours. We all have days that just don't turn out like we expected and are faced with problems that are beyond our control. It's the challenges that change us into who God created us to be. God has a purpose for the pain. He doesn't cause pain, but because of it, you will never be the same. The storms and struggles of life will make you stronger. "Winners never quit and quitters never win." Our attitude toward a situation can make it better or worse. Always remember, "This too shall pass." So again, it's up to you. You can be

_____

_____

_____

_____

_____

_____

The bright side is sunshine after the rain, joy through the pain and happiness to gain.

Ten years through the storms of life, the storms made me, and my faith stronger. Ten years later, I am blessed beyond what I deserve. Ten years into the future, God has a purpose and a plan and I will exalt Him!

Yes, He does love me. Yes, He does love YOU!

I asked Him to me show me His love when I searched the scriptures; God gave me a precious verse that I call one of my favorites! In Jeremiah 31:3 God says He loves YOU *"with an EVERLASTING love"*! He loves *ME "with an EVERLASTING love!"* There is no one else in your lifetime who will love you like He does!!

We may not always understand why things happen the way they do, but no matter what you are going through, HIS LOVE will carry you through, if you let it!

This too shall pass!

There is life after suffering! There is nothing too hard for God to handle! He is telling you today, "I am here for you my precious child!" "I LOVE YOU, my precious daughter!" "Tell Me, you LOVE ME!" "Praise My name today!" When was the last time you told your Father in Heaven how much you love Him? He desires to hear it as well!

My love and my hope come from the Lord! He loves me with an everlasting love! His love is a love that will never leave me, will never hurt me, and will always be faithful to me! He is GOD! Praise Him and thank Him for His love! His love is enough for today! He is drawing you to Him with His unfailing kindness! He loves YOU with an everlasting love! Everlasting, and for always! This is the love of Jesus!!

> *"The Lord appeared to us in the past, saying: "I have loved you with an everlasting love; I have drawn you with unfailing kindness." Jeremiah 31:3 (NIV)*
>
> *"For this reason I kneel before the Father,... I pray that out of his glorious riches he may strengthen you with power through*

Joy is a treasure hidden,
discovered in the pages of Scripture;
which will lead to the rewards
awaiting you.

the cross and took the nails for you and me! They are the beautiful hands of Jesus!

When you know that Jesus is holding your heart, ask Him to protect it and help you know who to trust with your heart. Let Him lead your relationships. The Bible has many boundaries set in place because God provides guidelines to help us live our life. It's when we go outside of His boundaries, we get ourselves in trouble and set ourselves up for hurt.

> *"May the God of hope fill you with all joy and peace as you trust in him, so that you may overflow with hope by the power of the Holy Spirit." Romans 15:13 (NIV)*

Who does have the control in your life?

I hate to say it, but I have let other people control me. I dare say I'm not alone in this. I didn't even see it, but my mom did. When I was married to my first husband, I gave him control over my emotions, my feelings, my heart and soul. I let him hold my heart as most spouses do and it just about destroyed me years later. Thankfully, God pulled me off the emotional roller coaster I was riding.

When we let other people dictate our emotions, by their words or actions to the point of anger, tears and fears, they have control over us. We may not even realize it because we are the ones being controlled. Notice, I said, when we "let other people." If you find yourself walking on eggshells around someone else, lying for them, or defending them, someone else is possibly controlling you. If that person makes you angry to the point you lose control of your temper and start yelling, someone else is possibly controlling you. We can become co-dependent when we are around someone who moves us to an action that we probably would not do otherwise. This person may have a controlling personality or an impossible temper or demeanor; they may be displaying manipulative or abusive behavior or may be addicted to drugs, alcohol or have another major addiction.

So, once again I want you to think, "Who has the control in your life?" If you need help getting out of a bad or dangerous situation,

_____

_____

_____

_____

_____

God has used my previous experiences dealing with a spouse with an addiction to help many other people. Please contact me through my website at **www.askgodtoday.com** if you would ever like to talk about options to help you cope with whatever you are going through.

5. Insert your name in the blanks and then read it as a prayer to God.

Dear Lord,

I pray God that You may fill _____ with all joy and peace as _____ trusts in You, so that _____ may overflow with hope by the power of the Holy Spirit. Thank You Lord. I love You. In Jesus name, I pray. Amen

Opening your hands and heart, letting go, and letting God, brings peace and joy to a hurting heart.

Wedding March as the beautiful bride makes her entrance, are you filled with gladness to the point of trying to contain the joyful tears filling your eyes?

These are a few sounds that bring gratification to our hearts. What are some happy sounds for you?

Maybe it's Christmas music, or the thrilling squeal of someone you love opening a gift.

Or a happy sound to you is the sound of the airplane you are on, hitting the runway and landing safely.

Whatever that happy sound is, it usually brings joy to our heart and a smile to our face. We need more joy and laughter in our world!

Solomon, the man known as the "The wisest man who ever lived," shared truth in Ecclesiastes 7:14, *"When times are good, be happy; but when times are bad, consider this: God has made the one as well as the other. Therefore, no one can discover anything about their future."*

You may have good days and bad days, but take heart, the same God that gave you the good day will bring you through the bad one.

God designs good and prosperous days. These are the days we should give added thanks to our precious Lord, the Giver of all good gifts. We should rejoice from our overjoyed hearts. Treasure in your heart the memories of the happy days. Be joyful, be cheerful, and be thankful! Enjoy prosperity while you can and enjoy God's favor as He gives. Nevertheless, remember just as the sun doesn't shine all the time, there will be rain and storms that are also inevitable.

> *"A happy heart makes the face cheerful, but heartache crushes the spirit." Proverbs 15:13 (NIV)*

If you live long enough you will experience overwhelming times of hardship, loss and devastation. Nothing is certain in this life. Absolutely nothing. It's crazy how we want to blame God when things don't go according to our expectations. God made the good days, as

_____

_____

_____

_____

_____

_____

*Happy sounds bring joy to our heart
and a smile to our face.*

where the candlelight brought peace to my darkness. The problems didn't change or go away, but it would give me the "time out" I needed to help me face whatever I was dealt with next.

Breathe in...Breathe out!!

Have you ever had to just take a deep breath and exhale?

Jesus says, *"Come to me, all you who are weary and burdened, and I will give you rest. Take my yoke upon you and learn from me, for I am gentle and humble in heart, and you will find rest for your souls. For my yoke is easy and my burden is light."* Matthew 11:28-30 (NIV)

Sometimes, we need to get a different perspective on whatever is causing fear, anger or the discontent in our lives. We have to make sure we don't say something we will later regret. When daily life doesn't seem to be going our way and we have too much on our to-do list and not enough time to do it in, we can ask God to help us see through His perspective. Ask Him to give you strength to handle the task at hand. Ask God to help you see people through His eyes. He loves us all, even the co-worker, friend, or family member who is causing the drama. Ask God to help you calm down and relax. He loves you!

Next time there is just too much drama, remember the slogan "Easy Does It"!

Pray for simple, straightforward, distinct, and uncomplicated ways of handling the "does it" part of this slogan. There are things we have to do when faced with challenging people. God will show you the way. Take care of yourself and keep your eyes on Jesus.

Application:

1. Who are the people, or what are the things that are causing unrest in your spirit and drama in your life?

_____
_____
_____

Day 21   *"I think I can, I think I can, I think I can."*

Do you ever feel overwhelmed, overworked, overlooked?

We are called to overcome!

Do you believe you can? "The Little Engine That Could," written by Watty Piper, was a well-known children's story, which tells the story of a little engine that had to pull a long line of freight cars. The little engine said "I can't; that is too much of a pull for me." But, after excuses were made, the little engine decided to pull the freight. As it started up the grade, the little engine started puffing and saying, "I think I can, I think I can, I think I can." When the little engine reached the top, the load started getting easier, then as it headed down the other side, the little engine began congratulating itself by saying, "I thought I could, I thought I could."

Ask God to help you not give up. Ask God to transform your mind so you "think you can." Our lives are busy. Every hour, every week, every month and every year, we are faced with day-to-day life. As I write this now, I am going into the busy time of my insurance business and closing the year out by helping people choose their insurance plans for the next year. The holidays are right around the corner where we will encounter the busy hustle and bustle of Christmas parties, and family gatherings. Then the New Year begins and we settle in for a long winter. We will then be quickly approaching the end of the school year. It's just life! Our calendars fill up quickly and we wonder how in the world we will get it all accomplished. Nevertheless, it gets done. We always make it through, don't we?

I have learned over the years that we ALWAYS make it through. No matter how hard the pain, the problem or the task ahead is...we always make it through!

but remember, God will give you the strength.

What a privilege. What a blessing!

So as we approach this season in our life, remember summer is right around the corner! Seek the One who will give you the strength to climb that hill that is in front of you, saying "I think I can, I think I can, I think I can."

As you start down the other side, you will look back and say "I thought I could, I thought I could!"

Allow me to pray for you today.

Dear Lord,

Thank You for all your blessings! Thank You for all the privileges that we have been given! Give us the strength to face the hills we have to climb. Help us remember You are climbing them with us. We can't give up now! We know our work will one day be rewarded and we thank You Lord. I lift my sweet friends up to You. I pray You will bless them today and everyday with Your harvest of blessings.
In Jesus name I pray!

Amen.

Application:

1. Write down your to-do list for today and approach one task at a time.

✓	To-Do Item
____	_____
____	_____
____	_____
____	_____
____	_____

Week Four

No Matter What

Day 22   Give Away Today!

Wow, it's our last week together. Time sure flies when you're having fun. (I do hope you're having fun.) We have covered a lot during these last three weeks. God laid "Joy Beyond" on my heart to share my struggles with others and help people know we can have joy even beyond the struggles of life. Life is not easy, and can be very hard at times, but when we seek the Giver of life and keep our eyes on Jesus, **joy is within reach and obtainable.**

Is it really better to give than receive?

"Give away today, like tomorrow won't come" are the words from a Charles Billingsley song. Is it really better to give than receive? What are you holding on to which could really be a blessing to someone else? When I had an opportunity recently to tell my son, "it is better to give than receive," I started thinking about the word, give. Jesus was the individual who said, "It is more blessed to give than to receive."

To attain joy, bestow joy on others!

What can we do to make the world we live in just a little better? How can we let God use us? I want my life to reflect Christ, and what better example than the One who gave His all!

In America, we are blessed and are rich in the eyes of the world. Therefore, what do we have that we can provide, or give away to bless someone else? First, we can give away more smiles and laughter. We can brighten up someone's day just by smiling at him or her.

When was the last time you had a deep-down inside belly laugh that brought tears to your eyes or made you snort aloud? Laugh. We all need laughter. It is a stress reliever. We all need to lighten up

"Every good and perfect gift is from above and comes down from the Father." God so loved the world, HE GAVE! God is the Master giver! He gave His only son; He graciously gives forgiveness, even when we don't deserve it. He bestows on us His strength, wisdom, clarity, and discernment. He pours out His love, joy, peace, happiness all over us until it starts seeping over into the lives of those around us. He provides us THIS day and our daily bread. God has given us spiritual gifts and abilities to use to help build His kingdom. God gives and gives! We need to always let Jesus be our example.

So, do you want to be more like Jesus?

Look around you and see where you can be His hands and feet and be a blessing and GIVE!

> *"And I have been a constant example of how you can help those in need by working hard. You should remember the words of the Lord Jesus: 'It is more blessed to give than to receive.'"* Acts 20:35 (NLT)

> *"Every good and perfect gift is from above, coming down from the Father of the heavenly lights, who does not change like shifting shadows."* James 1:17 (NIV)

> *"Give, and it will be given to you. A good measure, pressed down, shaken together and running over, will be poured into your lap. For with the measure you use, it will be measured to you."* Luke 6:38 (NIV)

I recently read a devotion by Joyce Meyer about giving and wanted to share it with you here. *"God gave His only Son to free us, and while we can never equal that sacrifice, we must give back to Him in a way that means something. King David said he would not give God something that cost him nothing. I have learned that **true giving is not giving until I can feel it.** Giving away the clothes and household items I'm finished with may be a nice gesture, but it doesn't equal real giving. **Real giving occurs when I give somebody something that I want to keep."***

He gives strength, wisdom, clarity, discernment and a sound mind.

"The LORD gives strength to his people; the LORD blesses his people with peace." Psalm 29:11 (NIV)

"If any of you lacks wisdom, you should ask God, who gives generously to all without finding fault, and it will be given." James 1:5 (NIV)

He gives us love, joy, peace and happiness.

"But God, being rich in mercy, because of the great love with which he loved us, even when we were dead in our trespasses, made us alive together with Christ—by grace you have been saved…." Ephesians 2:4–5 (NIV)

"Now may the Lord of peace himself give you peace at all times and in every way. The Lord be with you all." 2 Thessalonians 3:16 (NIV)

He gives us THIS day and our daily bread.

"Give us today our daily bread." Matthew 6:11 (NIV)

God has given us spiritual gifts and abilities to be used to help build His kingdom.

"A spiritual gift is given to each of us so we can help each other. To one person the Spirit gives the ability to give wise advice; to another the same Spirit gives a message of special knowledge. The same Spirit gives great faith to another, and to someone else the one Spirit gives the gift of healing. He gives one person the power to perform miracles, and another the ability to prophesy. He gives someone else the ability to discern whether a message is from the Spirit of God or from another spirit. Still another person is given the ability to speak in unknown languages, while another is given the ability to interpret what is being said. It is the one and only Spirit who distributes all these gifts. He alone decides which gift each person should have." (1 Corinthians 12:7-11 NIV)

Day 23   *My own little "pity party"*

As I sat there having my own little "pity party," I realized once again how much I needed the Lord.

Daily I need His love, His comfort, and I need His touch.

Instead of being "touched by an angel," I need to be touched by the Master Healer, Jesus! Sometimes, especially as women, we let the world swallow us up with doubt, loneliness, insecurity and sometimes even hopelessness. We feel we just cannot seem to get it right, no matter how hard we try.

For the most part, life doesn't usually pull me down too much and I feel I have it all together. I am not a person who usually mopes around feeling sorry for myself. Occasionally there are family or financial worries. Some of my main **"joy zappers"** are when there is more month than money, or the kids make a wrong choice. Physical pain can certainly cause the loss of joy.

I have my hand and my heart in many things. However, even those of us who have complete trust in the Lord, at times have moments of doubt. I am who I say I am, and I do what I say I am going to do. I don't just talk the talk, I try to walk the walk. When things go wrong, as they sometimes do, **I usually cry** for a few minutes and stuff it down deep inside of me. Only God, and my husband (if it doesn't involve him), and maybe one or two friends who will pray for me know what is happening.

Can I get a witness?

"Then he touched her, and instantly she could stand straight. How she praised God!" Luke 13:13 (NLT)

"Then he touched their eyes and said, "Because of your faith, it will happen." Matthew 9:29 (NLT)

"When Jesus arrived at Peter's house, Peter's mother-in-law was sick in bed with a high fever. But when Jesus touched her hand, the fever left her. Then she got up and prepared a meal for him." Matthew 8:14, 15 (NLT)

I am a survivor.

I am a real live transparent survivor! I am a breast cancer survivor! I am a divorce survivor! I am a heart attack survivor! It reminds me of the song that says, "I am woman, hear me roar." I roar only for the sake of Christ. He is my Savior! He saved me for a purpose, and I will keep telling others what He has done for me until the day I die and I meet Him face to face!

"For to you it has been granted for Christ's sake, not only to believe in Him, but also to suffer for His sake..." Philippians 1:29 (NASB)

We don't have to share all the details. Nobody really needs to know everything. However, sometimes when you do share, you may just find you are not alone. There may be some sweet young teenager going through a time of loneliness, or a single mom who can't pay all her bills, who needs the touch of the Master. Someone may be reading this who doubts his or her worth and may even feel like ending it all. I am here to tell you, there is nothing that Jesus cannot fix, change, heal or improve. He wants to touch your life. Then He wants a relationship with you. He will take away your loneliness, He will help you find a way to pay all the bills and He says, "You are worthy."

2. Didn't you feel a little silly when it was over?

_____

_____

_____

3. How did you bring yourself out of it?

_____

_____

_____

4. What do you think you can do the next time you have the joy zapped right out of you and fall into this zap trap Satan uses against us?

_____

_____

_____

5. Try the following things:

    1. Pray, asking God to give you a scripture.
    2. Open your Bible and read it.
    3. Then, practice what we have been doing during the past 23 days and write your name in the places that apply. Pray again and ask God to touch you with His comfort, His strength and His love! Ask God to help you overcome the doubt, the loneliness or the insecurity you are feeling. Ask God to use you to help and encourage others, by sharing what He has done in your life with them.

Have you been touched by the Master?

The Master's touch turns our pain to joy, our joy turns to faith, and our faith touches others.

Pure Joy

> *"Consider it pure joy, my brothers and sisters, whenever you face trials of many kinds, because you know that the testing of your faith produces perseverance. Let perseverance finish its work so that you may be mature and complete, not lacking anything." James 1:2-4 (NIV)*

Proclaimed in chapter 1 of James in the Bible, *"Whenever you face trials, you should consider it pure joy."* Now, I don't know about you, but **it's hard** to be joyful when you are in the midst of a trial or hardship. During this time, we need to be seeking God and asking Him to show us how to consider the trial or hardship, as pure joy. Because, we aren't just to consider it joy, but pure joy. Pure joy comes from God. Pure means it is free from any contaminates from the world. This is God's joy! **God's joy is pure joy!** He gives His joy to those people who choose to seek Him and live for Him. He wants us all to experience pure joy. This pure joy is the only way you can persevere through a trial and come out making progress for the purpose of the Kingdom of God. When God gives pure joy, God gets the glory!

When we walk in the light of Christ and live for the Lord, we find joy in our heart. It doesn't always feel like joy, as I have explained. If, when going through the fiery trials of life, you allow God to burn off all the sinful impurities, He will bring purity into your heart. This purity, whether felt or not, turns your pain to joy. It's not something we can do, or even make happen. We do, however, have choices, whether to allow God to purify us and refine us to become more like Christ or walk in pride and think we can continue to do it our way. God doesn't force Himself on you. He is a gentleman. He knocks at the door of your heart and waits for you to invite Him into the furnace with you. It's during this refining that God reveals Himself in a more intimate way.

Perseverance Finished

It is through the trials of life when our faith is tested. The testing of our faith over a period produces perseverance. The perseverance produces in us maturity and then we become complete and identified as a child of God. The work God began in you and the trials He allowed

Please allow me to end this day by praying for you.

Dear Heavenly Father,

I praise You and love You! I stand in awe of who You are and what You mean to me, and to each of the people reading and praying this prayer with me. God, You allow us to go through trials for a purpose and a reason. I pray if there is anyone reading this who is going through a trial of any kind right now, You would pour Your grace and love out on them. Reveal yourself to them Lord, and help them trust You during this season in their life. Carry them Lord; embrace them with Your presence and help them see the pure joy, which only comes from knowing You and living for You! As we make progress Lord in our day-to-day lives, help us to persevere knowing You are finishing the work You began in us. In Jesus name, I pray. Amen.

When you can't see the light at the end of the tunnel, the darkness of the tunnel is overcome by the light of Jesus!

has devastated me. **I have said, "I don't know if I can even make it another day" when feeling the dread of facing tomorrow.** Most of us have had some sort of sorrow and pain happen in our lives, which overwhelmed us with despair.

But my God says, *"Do not lose hope. Don't be afraid. Do not lose heart."* He is the God of new beginnings. He is the God of HOPE!

> *"Therefore we do not lose heart. Though outwardly we are wasting away, yet inwardly we are being renewed day by day. For our light and momentary troubles are achieving for us an eternal glory that far outweighs them all."*
> *2 Corinthians 4:16, 17 (NIV)*

As the story goes...the Israelites soon forgot what the Lord had done for them and started grumbling in the desert. Does that sound familiar? We praise God while things are good and then we start whining when things are not so good. Therefore, God had to show them again His power by sending manna and quail to fill their stomachs.

When I was going through cancer, **I was not a Christian.** I THOUGHT I was. I did pray, but had never accepted Christ into my heart. My hope was more in the prayers of others and in the doctors and the treatment. It was later, when I committed my life to the Lord that I understood God's grace and provision in my life.

When I went through my divorce, after a long four years of counseling for our marriage and my husband's addiction problems and his struggles, I did finally have hope. I knew the Lord, and He knew me. I had grown close to the Lord by seeking Him through prayer, His Word and godly people. I knew He had a purpose for the suffering and the pain I was enduring. **Never is it God's will for people to divorce.** Nevertheless, according to the Bible, He will allow it under certain circumstances. That doesn't make it easier. However, during this time, my hope was found in Christ, family, friends and others.

before it was final, knowing I had done everything I could have possibly done to salvage the marriage. I am thankful for godly counselors and their wisdom and discernment to counsel me. If you are going through desperate times and need counsel, seek godly counsel through your church and Christian counseling. There is hope through hardship.

God gave me Hope through my kids.

I have two beautiful kids and they are now 23 and 19, but at the start of my divorce, they were only 12 and 7. They were precious and I poured my life into my kids. Especially at Christmas, I might have gone a little overkill trying to make it up to the kids what they had lost after the divorce. They would keep me smiling and love me with their hugs. My seven-year old son would sleep with me and I loved it! My kids gave me hope and strength to keep on keeping on! They needed me and I needed them!

God gave me Hope through my parents.

God gave me two wonderful parents and I miss them desperately. I think of them almost every day. They have gone home to be with the Lord. My dad was my rock and my mom always lent a listening ear, and if you know me, I like to talk!! My dad taught me to look at life through rose-colored glasses and to set goals always! Rest in peace, Mom and Dad. I love and miss you!

God gave me Hope through my siblings.

During my breast cancer my sister was my hero! She lives in Florida. However, when I had to have surgery for cancer, she came and stayed with me all day and all night at the hospital. She kept me encouraged. My brother has carried on our family name. I am blessed to have such a wonderful sister and brother.

God gave me Hope through friends.

I had wonderful Christian friends who came alongside me and prayed with me. They helped me cut my hilly yard, paint my kitchen,

As God parted the Red Sea for the Israelites to cross through on dry land, He will do the same for us. He led them to freedom. He made a way far beyond what they would have ever imagined. God can part the sea of despair and discouragement in your life and lead you through on dry ground. He brings hope when things look hopeless.

"But as for you, be strong and do not give up…"
2 Chronicles 15:7a (NIV)

"As for me, I will always have hope; I will praise you more and more." Psalm 71:14 (NIV)

Application:

Say a prayer. Ask God to help you trust Him, even in the hard and discouraging times of your life. Ask Him to bring you hope through His Word and prayer, today. God can part the sea of despair and discouragement in your life. Ask Him to help you believe He will do this for you and to lead you through the circumstance you are currently in. Close your prayer by asking God to help you come out the other side exalting and singing His praises! Praise God for being the God of joy!

1. Write down the people and activities in your life that have brought you hope, like I have done in today's lesson. Write down how God has brought you hope through the following:

Bible_____

Prayer_____

Church_____

Spouse _____

Parents _____

Kids _____

Friends_____

Career_____

Day 26   Joy Zappers

Satan is always there to steal your joy, and God is always there to supply you with joy!

Whom are you going to allow to have their way in your life? Jesus made a way for us to overcome and have abundant joy.

> *"So you have sorrow now, but I will see you again; then you will rejoice, and no one can rob you of that joy." John 16:22 (NLT)*

I have discussed over the last several weeks some of the things in my life that rocked my world and stole my joy. Life is just plain hard sometimes.

Today we are going to look at what I call "Joy Zappers." Tomorrow, we are going to look more closely at how to clean up the clutter in our lives so we can allow God to supply us with His joy and peace.

Joy Zappers

Money or the lack thereof	Debt	Grief
Greed	Worries	Fear
Sickness	Problems	Frustrations
Pressure	Marriage	Stress
People / Relationships	Parents	Negativity
Kids	Job	Thoughts
Addictions	Pain	Challenges
Sin	Disappointments	School
Insecurities	Other:	

Abundant Joy

> *"Oh, give me back my joy again; you have broken me—now let me rejoice." Psalm 51:8 (NLT)*

In 2 Corinthians 7:4, Paul said these words, *"I am greatly encouraged; in all our troubles my joy knows no bounds."* Now that is abundant joy, a joy that knows no bounds. I hope to come to the place in my life where even in all my troubles, I have abundant joy. Life may knock us down for a moment, but we can get back up again with joy in our heart and joy in our spirit.

God restores! Do you believe it?

> *"Though you have made me see troubles, many and bitter, you will restore my life again; from the depths of the earth you will again bring me up." Psalm 71:20 (NIV)*

A Thorn in my Flesh

Sometimes God will allow us to have troubles and hardships in order to show us who He is. It is when we are weak that He is made strong. His grace is sufficient! Paul set us a great example and said, *"That is why, for Christ's sake, I delight in my weaknesses, in insults, in hardships, in persecutions and in difficulties."* It is all for the sake of Christ! If we delight in our weaknesses then God will show us His power and we will delight in His power. He will turn that delight in Him to joy in our heart.

> *"Therefore, in order to keep me from becoming conceited, I was given a thorn in my flesh, a messenger of Satan, to torment me. Three times I pleaded with the Lord to take it away from me. But he said to me, 'My grace is sufficient for you, for my power is made perfect in weakness.' Therefore I will boast all the more gladly about my weaknesses, so that Christ's power may rest on me. That is why, for Christ's sake, I delight in weaknesses, in insults, in hardships, in persecutions, in difficulties. For when I am weak, then I am strong."*
> *2 Corinthians 12:7-10 (NIV)*

4. Now, write a prayer asking God how serious is this problem and ask Him what you can do to handle it or make it different.

_____

_____

_____

_____

_____

_____

_____

5. Fill in the blanks with your name and then read it back aloud.

"Therefore, in order to keep _____ from becoming conceited, _____ was given a thorn in _____'s flesh, a messenger of Satan, to torment _____. Three times _____ pleaded with the Lord to take it away from _____. But he said to _____, "My grace is sufficient for _____, for my power is made perfect in weakness." Therefore I will boast all the more gladly about _____'s weaknesses, so that Christ's power may rest on _____. That is why, for Christ's sake, _____ delights in weaknesses, in insults, in hardships, in persecutions, in difficulties. For when _____ is weak, then _____ is strong." 2 Corinthians 12:7-10 (NIV)

6. NOW, TRUST HIM!! This too shall pass!!

A life living with abundant joy, is a life giving to God the things that destroy.

some we gave away to charity and some we just straightened up and put away in its rightful place.

It's the same with our personal life. Some things we need to throw away. We need to get rid of all the sin that is preventing us from being the person God has called us to be - whether it be anger, jealousy, gossip, overindulgence, greed, pride or any other sin that has entangled us. God has a plan for our life, but we often allow sin to get in the way of His plan. We then wonder why God doesn't bless us. He is ready and willing to help us sort through everything in our lives if we will invite Him to do it. We need to ask ourselves, "What am I hanging on to that I need to get rid of?"

When I first became a believer in Christ I didn't really feel like I had any major sin in my life. I was a mom of a four year old and a newborn. I worked a fulltime job, came home and took care of my family, cooked dinner and watched television and went to bed. I had never committed adultery, or murdered anyone and I thought those were the major sins in life. Therefore, I thought I was good. I became a believer in Christ because I was looking for what God could do for me. Later I understood how selfish my faith was in the beginning. God was working on my heart and revealing Himself to me and my heart started softening. I realized I had never asked Christ to be my Savior. I believe my real major sin was my unbelief. I needed forgiveness for not believing Jesus was the Son of God. After studying God's Word and hearing more and more messages, I knew I was a sinner in need of forgiveness. Jesus was the only One who could forgive me and change me. He loved me through the cross.

It might just be that you need to de-clutter.

The only way to eliminate the sin in our lives is to run into the arms of Jesus. Someone told me recently, the only way she can let go of the sin in her life is to "run to His love." She said, "When I know His love and I find my delight in Him, I don't want the sin anymore, or it becomes a non-issue because I am so consumed with Him." When we fill ourself up with more of Christ, He changes our desires and we have more of a desire to please Him. We want to lay down the old life and pick up the new life.

The God of Peace

"For God is not a God of disorder but of peace..."
1 Corinthians 14:33 (NIV)

God does not add disorder or confusion to people's lives. He brings peace. Therefore, if your life is full of clutter and disorder, it's time to reevaluate to see what changes need to be made. In this situation by relating cleaning up the clutter of a room in comparison to cleaning up the sins in our life, change is never easy and most people don't want to change. People are afraid of change, especially when it involves the unknown of the future. When we don't know what the future will look like, we tend to stick with things we are familiar with. So, if we are avoiding what really needs to be done, we need to step back and look at what we can do to make our situation different. It requires doing what is hard at times, and putting down the things which are displeasing to the Lord. Nevertheless, the outcome is phenomenal and God can give you a brand new start. He can bring peace, love, joy and beauty into your life. He has great plans to give you a new hope and future.

Many times people don't want to become a Christian because they think there are too many rules and God won't let them do anything. So, they justify their actions and keep on living the life they are living. I can relate. I didn't want to be a Christian. I remember specifically rejecting the Lord at a youth event when I was in Middle School. I didn't want to be a "Jesus Freak." I thought it was boring and you couldn't do anything. I also hear people say they don't believe in God because He didn't answer their prayers. God doesn't want us to just try Him out to see if He works for us. He wants us to commit our whole life to Him. I am living proof that He does answer prayers. It is prideful to think we can do things our way and only call on God when we need Him in a time of crisis. The peace and joy are available for us, all we have to do is receive them.

God is the only one who can help us make the changes in our life that can put a halt to the snowball effect. He knows we can become overwhelmed with life. He knows we don't even know where to start sometimes. It's the same with cleaning out a closet...we think - where do I even begin? One thing, one step, ONE DAY at a time!! If we begin with one garbage bag, make a stack for the things we want to give away, and clean out a closet, then changes will begin. Likewise, if we will get out our Bible, and buy a journal and make a list of what we need to change in our life, that is a good beginning. Then we add prayer to the equation, trust in God, and let Him lead us. Most of all let Him add light from His Holy Spirit to change us. He just wants a willing heart. He will de-clutter all the junk in our lives that we need to get rid of, and motivate us to shine brightly for Him.

God is not a God of disorder. He is a God of peace. He says that we should strive to be like Christ; therefore, we need to be sure that everything is done in a fitting and orderly manner. We have to keep taking one step at a time and one day at a time. We have to do a little work that may not always be easy and leave the progress to Him. One day you will look back and see where God changed you. The old is gone and the new is alive and well!

Application:

1. Write down a room or closet in your house that needs to be de-cluttered.

   _____

   _____

   _____

2. Set aside a day or a couple of hours to do it. Go ahead...look at your calendar and put it on your To-Do List to accomplish. Write your scheduled time down here.

   _____

   _____

_____

_____

_____

_____

_____

I am lifting you up right now as I write this and pray that God will help you clean up the clutter in your life, whether it is a closet, a whole room or a whole house. I am praying more importantly that if there is sin in your life, the God of Peace will bring change and peace to your heart and give you the desire to change the things that need to be changed so He will transform you into the Child of God He desires you to be.

God can turn your chaos to peace, your clutter to beauty, your old to new!

you. He won't betray you. He will protect you, He will provide for you and He will ALWAYS be present with you!

Amazingly, we can actually talk and walk with Jesus daily. We may not be able to see Him with our eyes, but we see Him as He hugs and loves us through others. He speaks to us through His Word and through godly people. He provides for us and protects us, even when we make bad choices. He calms our fears and our bitter hearts. He forgives us even when we don't deserve it. He forgets our sins, our unfaithfulness and our disobedience.

No more pain, no more tears, no more suffering!

He is God who came in the flesh and made a way for you and me to spend eternity in Heaven. In Heaven where there will be no more pain, no more tears, no more fear or evil. Just knowing that one day we will see Jesus face to face keeps me focused on His purposes and His plans. I hold on, knowing that this world is not all there is to life. When life gets tough, I look toward the heavens and know Jesus loves me!

Remain in His love!

Love comes from Heaven. Christ was filled with the love from the Father. He loved His son Jesus, and Jesus teaches us how to love others. He tells us that if we keep His commands and remain in His love, just as Jesus did, than His joy will be in us and our joy will be complete.

John 15:9-11 in the Bible says, "As the Father has loved me, so have I loved you. Now remain in my love. If you keep my commands, you will remain in my love, just as I have kept my Father's commands and remain in his love. I have told you this so that my joy may be in you and that your joy may be complete." (NIV)

Do you desire to have joy in your heart? It's plain and simple: keep the commands of the Lord and remain in His love. The closer we stay to God and His love, the more desire we have to keep His commands.

Saved.

Before I believed with my heart that Jesus brings eternal life, I had heard people talk about being "saved" but had no idea what it even meant. When you are "saved" you have become a believer in Christ, believing He died on the cross over 2000 years ago. You have asked Him to forgive you and "save" you from your sins. When He saves you from your sins, you are guaranteed eternal life after physical death because of the blood that Jesus shed on the cross the day He died. After I got saved and forgiven, God started changing me. The old me was gone and I became a new person. My desires started changing. I no longer wanted to party and I had a strong hunger to learn more about who this Jesus was. I remember praying and asking God, "If You want me to know who Jesus is, God, You are going to have to reveal Him to me." I had heard of Jesus because I celebrated Christmas and Easter (mostly for Santa Claus and the Easter Bunny). It occurred to me after committing my life to Him that He was in my head, but not in my heart. I honestly never really knew Him. **When you move Jesus from your head to your heart, then you move from death to life.** You are saved!

Fruits of the Spirit.

Galatians 5 tells us what the fruits of the Spirit are, *"So I say, walk by the Spirit, and you will not gratify the desires of the flesh. But the fruit of the Spirit is love, JOY, peace, forbearance, kindness, goodness, faithfulness, gentleness and self-control. Against such things there is no law."* Galatians 5:16, 22, 23 (NIV)

We have to seek the Lord in all His ways to obtain and live in joy. Searching for and striving to learn to live for Christ by bearing the fruits of the Spirit will clean up the clutter and the messiness in our life. My desire is that we all lay down the sins that so easily entangle and hinder us from pleasing the Lord and fulfilling His purpose in and through us.

I suppose if you are reading this sentence that you have made it all the way to day 28! Yay! Thank you for sharing your days with me. I

God, your Word is my delight. It fills me up day after day. I am far from perfect and I need forgiveness everyday from You and from those I have unknowingly hurt. My heart is pure and raw at this very moment and hurts deeply, my body feels overwhelmed with all I have been dealt. God, Your Word is healing and loving to my abandoned heart. Your Word guides me and gives me joy even in the hardest times. I was chosen to bear the name of You, Lord, and I will seek to bring You honor in all I do, even and especially through the times of tears. My heart is Yours! I love you Jesus.   (a day from my journal)

Joy can be found beyond the clutter of life when you seek the Cross-bearer who brings eternal life!

We sing the words of this Christmas song written by Isaac Watts every year at Christmas. "Joy to the World" is based on Psalm 98 in the Bible. Do we believe? Do you believe?

Our joy comes from Christ, the Savior of the world. Open your heart and prepare to give Him room to rule with truth and grace and reign in your life forever. His blessings flow…let heaven and nature sing. The glories of His righteousness and the wonders of His love will bring joy to your heart and soul. My prayer is you won't miss it.

"Joy to the world! The Lord is come
Let earth receive her King!
Let every heart prepare Him room
And heaven and nature sing

Joy to the world! The Savior reigns
Let men their songs employ
While fields and floods
Rocks, hills and plains
Repeat the sounding joy

Stories from the Heart

Contributors

God didn't answer my prayer right away about healing my dad but he eventually in His own time did. Through all of this God made my mom a stronger woman. She grew closer to God through this disaster. She has been an encouragement and a role model to me. I couldn't have asked for better parents or for my life to have been any different now.

God showed us joy, hope, and comfort during this hard time in our life.

Never give up on someone you think will never change. Our God is bigger and stronger than we can imagine!

was too difficult to deal with, kept causing problems, and would not do what I was told.

Therefore, on April 7, 2012, my parents had to make a very hard decision of sending me to a Christian Group Home called "House of Hope." I went that day unknowingly where I was going. My clothes and belongings were already packed and in the suitcase, in the back of the car.

I cried for three months and thought my parents would cave in and pull me out of the program, but they didn't. I hated them for putting me there. I had told them if they ever put me in a Girl's home, I would never speak to them again.

One day it hit me in the face...I needed help. I could not live as I was living anymore. I was hurting everyone who loved me, but mostly myself. I finally surrendered to God, fully this time. God started revealing Himself to me day after day.

I learned my parents didn't send me there because they didn't want me, but because they loved me. Once I saw that and accepted the fact that I was there to stay, I allowed God to change me. Things started getting better for me. I could actually sit down and have a conversation with my parents. I started moving up phases in the program and given more responsibilities to test me. I lived with seven other girls and it was hard not to argue, but through the fights, we became like sisters. They saw the good, bad and the ugly.

God started giving me words and speaking to me. That is when I really began to change. One night we were at a Bluegrass Christian concert and the man speaking was telling us how he had to get his band out of their little town for people to realize who they were and for their band to get any bigger. I heard the Lord at that moment tell me, "Hannah, I brought you out of your little town for you to find out who you are in Me." I boohooed and I was consumed by God's presence. I knew God had a plan for me and I finally understood He knew what He was doing, and that all I had to do was trust Him.

I continued to progress in my faith and in the phases towards graduating from the program. In June 2013, after 13 months I graduated. I was the 66th person out of 150 to graduate in eleven years. Some girls never do.

Experiencing Joy

Caryn Christensen

From the time I was born, and all through my growing up years, I suffered extreme hardships. When my brother and I were removed from our home as toddlers because of gross maternal neglect, we were placed in foster homes and reunited with our father several years later. It was in the foster homes that we were exposed to and became victims of physical and sexual abuse. When my father took custody of us, he had remarried and things were no better in our new blended family. Both parents were physically and emotionally abusive, to the point where, as a young teen, I tried to commit suicide just to escape the relentless emotional pain that gnawed at my insides day and night. When my attempt failed, only then did I receive the support I needed from the court system as they sought out a permanent living place for me. Had it not been for a great aunt who God used as a conduit to find me a safe foster home, I would not be here today.

So it would seem incongruent to be talking about joy. You might be wondering how and where joy comes into a story such as mine? Or yours? How do you lay claim to such a grand and glorious thing as joy when it has been stripped from you because of your circumstances, many times through no fault of your own? How do you move from knowing the word in your head to *experiencing* it within your heart?

I can tell you in four words. Joy is a choice. It also takes lots of hard work. In fact, you may have to fight for it like I did. You may be thinking, "Wait, shouldn't I just *have* joy because I'm a Christian?" Yes and no. Galatians 5:22 tells us joy is a fruit of the Spirit. I believe when someone asks the Lord into their heart, the Holy Spirit takes up residence there and plants the *seeds* of His image, more commonly known as the fruit of the Spirit. Within that seed lies all the *potential* for growth and maturity. That is where choice and hard work comes in. Our part is to make sure that seed is planted in the fertile soil of an open heart towards the Lord, watered with God's word and tended to with prayer. So whether you *feel* it or not, at that point, God's joy is now yours. It won't be mature yet, but joy is there.

The Summer I was Twelve

Ken Mayfield

My earliest memories are of our home, where there were many struggles. My dad became an alcoholic when I was very young. His lifestyle included having numerous affairs, disappearing for days while drunk or with one of his many girlfriends. When he was at home, he was very abusive. Once when I was nine, he bent my mother's hand backwards until he had broken every bone in her hand. He then laughed and mocked her saying, there was no way she could drive herself to the hospital.

The summer I turned 12 was one of the worst. By then, my dad had returned home for a few months but was still drinking heavily. Our car had been repossessed and we were living in a rented, run-down mobile home in the outskirts of Charlotte, N.C. My parents discovered that my mom was pregnant. Dad was not happy. On August 3rd, he came home and with slurred, drunken speech, announced that he wasn't going to have another baby. He stated that he was going to take my mother into the bedroom and kill her. He began beating her and throwing her around the small trailer's living room. When she was on the floor, he kicked her so forcefully that each kick thrust her body forward on the floor and then into the narrow hallway leading to the bedroom at the end of the hall. Afraid, I ran to my bedroom and grabbed a .410 gauge shotgun, a gift from the previous Christmas, since I loved to hunt. As my dad passed the doorway, I told him to stop. Mom was still crumpled on the floor. Dad was holding her wrists, still kicking her with each step. I was in the corner of the room with the gun pointed at my dad. He dropped my mother's wrists and walked toward me. The next thing I remember is seeing smoke roll from the end of the barrel of the gun, blood splatter everywhere, my dad grabbed his face and then fell forward on my feet. I ran from the room. In minutes many neighbors, the police, an ambulance and TV crews arrived.

My mom and I were taken to the Juvenile Division of the Mecklenburg County (Charlotte) Police Department. We sat in a room with two detectives for hours telling of past events with my dad and

While I know that God has brought me a long way, I know that I am nothing without Him. I am so blessed and undeserving of the goodness that He has shown me.

"And if it seem evil unto you to serve the Lord, choose you this day whom ye will serve...but as for me and my house, we will serve the Lord." Joshua 24:15

Ken Mayfield
Associate Pastor
Mountain View Baptist Church
Spartanburg, SC
You can contact Ken at: Kenmayfield01@aol.com

JOY is not just happiness. Joy evolves as you grow stronger in your walk with the LORD. I was so fortunate to have friends who gave me Christian guidance. I did not allow myself to get wrapped up in self-pity, anger or revenge. Staying involved in the church and a Divorce Care group, allowed me to see that I was not alone and I did not have to continue to be a part of the devil's triangle. I had grown closer to the Lord as I struggled in my marriage. I knew that my strength came only from God, and that He would never leave me. I knew that God was always with me in mind, body, and spirit. As trouble came, I was on my knees seeking God's will. Those nights on my knees with tears flowing down my face taught me grace. It actually changed me on the inside and outside. I had to hold my head up and continue to follow God's path, not the world's.

I had found JOY! I was very happy and content. I had my plans to get my children out of college and I was going to join the Peace Corps and travel wherever it took me. I was not looking to date or consider marriage, ever. (My friends will vouch for that). I was living my life joyfully.

God had His plans for me and my family. I met and married a wonderful Christian father of three boys and we blended our family together. I love the LORD, I love my family, and I love my life. I have joy in my heart!!!!!!!!!!!!!

the next months we grieved over what she might not be able to do in life. And then God gave us a bigger wake-up call.

Savannah was born on September 18, 2000. She was the most beautiful thing I'd ever seen. But our prayers for a miracle had not been answered, and indeed, she was born without a left leg. In its place was a large open sore and a twisted malformation along what should have been her left thigh. She was taken to the NICU for observation and for testing to rule out possibilities. Finally, doctors came to the conclusion that she had been born with a large "teratoma" tumor in her pelvis, hip and leg; it had been growing there since the first seven weeks after conception. Although most Teratomas are benign, a biopsy taken 6 days after she was born showed that our baby's tumor was malignant. Our little girl had cancer.

One of my darkest but most vivid memories of that time was sitting in a rocking chair in the hospital, rocking Savannah and waiting for the doctors to explain what a Teratoma was and what the treatment would be, and suddenly being so overwhelmed with grief and fear that I looked straight up to the heavens and yelled out, "WHERE-IS-GOD???"

To be honest, my relationship with God to that point had been a lot like having a personal shopper. I gave Him my list of things I needed or wanted, and He either came through on them or made it clear the item wasn't available at the time...I'd have to come back later with more bargaining power. I was capable and strong and independent; I'd been successful and in control of my own life. Until now. Now every single thing that was happening was completely out of my hands. And I hated it.

As the treatments began (chemo at 10 days old, surgery at 2 weeks, major surgery at 5 months, major surgery at 13 months) my emotions went from shocked to devastated to depressed to angry to helpless to broken. It was a difficult, gut-wrenching year. Treatments made her sick and lose her hair, which might have happened anyway, but we had to hold her little arms and leg down for painful injections and IV lines and cleaning the open wound. I was a wreck. Every time we thought we'd reached a good treatment plan, a new wrench would be thrown in. After a 10-hour major surgery to remove the tumor at 5 months, the tumor grew back even bigger over the summer. In

Fear not, for I have redeemed you; I have summoned you by name; you are Mine.

> "When you pass through the waters, I will be with you,
> and when you pass through the rivers, they will not sweep over
> you.
> When you walk through the fire, you will not be burned,
> the flames will not set you ablaze.
> For I am the Lord, your God, the Holy One, your Savior."
> Isaiah 43:1-3

I'm not going to pretend everything was peachy after that. The surgery lasted 13 hours, and the recovery was difficult, but we recovered, and there was a constant peace. And I'm not going to act all rosy and tell you that having a child with a physical disability is always exactly easy. There have been hard things we've endured: follow-up surgeries, learning to walk with crutches, falling on slick floors, ignorant comments and the staring...good grief, the adults are worse than the kids. It's not exactly fun growing up with one leg, although sometimes it can be, in a sick, twisted way. Like this spring, when we went to a baseball game for my 10-year-old son, and Savannah and I were walking to the stands when a little boy came running over to us. "What happened to your leg?" he repeated over and over again, circling her. "Where's your other leg? What happened to it?" Savannah very politely and sweetly bent toward the 4-year old little leaguer and said, "I didn't eat all my vegetables when I was little..." to which the boy dropped his jaw and his baseball glove on the ground and just stood there as she walked away smiling. The girl's got spunk, I tell you. God knew what He was doing. Savannah teaches me about resilience and perseverance and fight and joy every day.

My daughter just turned 13. She swam on the high school swim team this year as a seventh grader, a dream she's had since she started swimming at age 5. All those nights we worried about how she'd do this or that...she's got it covered. There's very little she can't do, when she sets her mind to it...she's stubborn, just like her Daddy.

U + H = JOY

Dwayne Morris

"Therefore if you have any encouragement from being united with Christ, if any comfort from his love, if any common sharing in the Spirit, if any tenderness and compassion, then make my joy complete by being like-minded, having the same love, being one in spirit and of one mind. Do nothing out of selfish ambition or vain conceit. Rather, in humility value others above yourselves, not looking to your own interests but each of you to the interests of the others." (Philippians 2:1-4)

The apostle Paul gives us a formula for joy: Unity + Humility = Joy.

Unity is an interesting dynamic. You might think it means you just conform to everything. You are afraid unity means you are a "Yes Man." But that's not the case. If you're looking for unity, then you're looking for the option that helps all parties involved. You want the win-win that will produce the best results. If not, then it can only lead to confusion and frustration.

I had the privilege of spending a day with a missionary who was on stateside assignment. He sent word that he wanted to tour local companies owned by Christian businessmen. I made a few calls and we were set for a day of tours.

One of our destinations was a small operation that had been around for several years. Their service was re-tooling a product that many of us use. They took old products, stripped them down and rebuilt them just like new. The owner was not able to meet us, but made arrangements for his "right-hand man" to show us around. This fellow was a simple man who was one of the first employees the owner had hired and who had helped the business become the success it is today. In essence the extent of his education was directly connected to his experience on the job over the years.

As we were beginning the tour, he took us to the place where their process began. He picked up a unit that needed work and began telling us how everything started. Seeing this used part and knowing it came from an existing product, my mind began to wonder where all of these parts came from in the United States or was this strictly a local

Standing in the distance, I stood there amazed that a thirteen year old would have the presence of mind to not relish in her victory and humble herself to serve her peers. Her humility was a tremendous expression of joy to those she encountered that morning.

Joy is described in many ways. I think Paul has it right in telling us that we can experience complete joy by striving to seek the best results for others and to humble ourselves to put them first. If we strive to build this trait in our lives, then we'll find ourselves more fulfilled and have a greater sense of purpose in our lives.

Dwayne Morris, blogger, speaker and author of "the Outrageous life"

Keep up with Dwayne:

blog: www.morrismatters.com
Twitter: @DwayneMorris
Facebook: www.facebook.com/dwaynemorris

I would stand by the six-inch window looking out for what seemed to be hours. Eventually a guard would walk by and look in through the glass. I asked for a Bible through the door and there was no response. This happened a few more times without any response. I realized the temperature was getting very hot and then very cold. This was how they tested you to show you what true discomfort felt like.

A few hours went by, the slot of my steel door opened, and they pushed a small Gideon's Bible under the door. It was extremely small and it was impossible to read without my eyeglasses. So I went through the motions of trying to ask the guard for a larger Bible without any success. As the temperature went from hot to cold and realizing I wouldn't be able to read the little Bible I began to become filled with depression.

The next emotion was crying my eyes out. I cried and cried like a little boy. When my tears stopped, and I couldn't cry any more, I picked up the little Bible. To my surprise, I was able to read the small print. I didn't realize the Lord heard my cry and restored my vision. I didn't need my eyeglasses and I was reading.

Psalm 107 : 19 – 20 NKJV "Then they cried out to the Lord in their trouble, and he saved them out of their distresses. He sent His Word and healed them and delivered them from their destructions."

The little Bible fell open to Acts chapter 16 and the title line read "Paul & Silas in Prison." I was extremely surprised to see that Paul and Silas were in prison just like me.

Acts 16 NLT: Paul and Silas in Prison

22 A mob quickly formed against Paul and Silas, and the city officials ordered them stripped and beaten with wooden rods. 23 They were severely beaten, and then they were thrown into prison. The jailer was ordered to make sure they didn't escape. 24 So the jailer put them into the inner dungeon and clamped their feet in the stocks.

25 Around midnight Paul and Silas were praying and singing hymns to God, and the other prisoners were listening. 26 Suddenly, there was a massive earthquake, and the prison was shaken to its foundations. All the doors immediately flew open, and the chains of every prisoner fell off! 27 The jailer woke up to see the prison doors wide open. He assumed the prisoners had escaped, so he drew his sword to kill

me. They put me back in the cell and I began to do the very same thing, I continued to sing and read the Bible.

The next morning the prison chaplain came to see me. He introduced himself and I enthusiastically told him when I get out of the hole in sixty days I wanted to come to the chapel services. He advised me that he spoke to the psychiatrist and I told him the same story. He looked into my eyes and smiled. He said "Simone, you keep doing exactly what you are doing."

This was my third day in the hole. Later that day one of the guards opened the door and I saw a bed roll on the floor. He commanded me to come out of the cell and he escorted me to the general population cell block.

Psalm 40:1 – 3 NLT: " I waited patiently on the Lord and he turned to me and heard my cry. He lifted me out of the mud and mire. He set my feet on solid ground as I walked along. He has given me a new song to sing a hymn of praise to our God. Many will see what he has done and be amazed. They will put their trust in the Lord."

I went out on the prison compound and realized that the Lord delivered me from that horrible hole. I went to the chapel services and began to learn the word of God. The Lord continued to guide me and protect me for the 25 months I was at Coleman. They provided me with seminary training and I received the favor of the chief jailor.

Genesis 39 21 – 23 KJV: "But the LORD was with Joseph, and showed him mercy, and gave him favour in the sight of the keeper of the prison. And the keeper of the prison committed to Joseph's hand all the prisoners that were in the prison; and whatsoever they did there, he was the doer of it. The keeper of the prison looked not to anything that was under his hand; because the LORD was with him, and that which he did, the LORD made it to prosper."

I found such joy even though I was in prison. During my time at Coleman I remembered how the Lord provided for me in the hole and I used the lesson I learned there to find peace and to be content in whatever situation I found myself.

I had grown very close to the chaplain, who became my mentor. Shortly before I was released he took me in his office and told me that from the very beginning he knew that the Lord had his hand on my life. He explained how I was released from the hole in three days. He

The HEART of Something New

Bill (Tiny) Bateman

As I sit at home watching the old year out, and the New Year in, I had just a few thoughts I decided to write down. Most of today and this week I have listened to, and read about many people ready for a New Year, a new start. Saying that 2013 was great or that it was the worst year they had ever had. Probably if I took enough time to worry about it I would have a little of each of those thoughts as well.

However, I can tell you that on June 4, 2003 when my Cardiologist walked into a room full of my family and fellow Ministers, he looked me in the eyes and said, "I'm sorry Mr. Bateman, but there is nothing we can do for you. Your heart is simply in a terminal condition and you won't live more than 3 days." I began truly living by the day and not year-by-year.

The fact is, you are a miracle. The fact that you have the breath to continue to go after your dreams, the fact that you have enough life to live another day, no matter how bad the days in the past actually were, is evidence enough that we shouldn't wish our days away waiting for better ones. Instead of waiting, we should continue to push for better days. Instead of wallowing in our pain, and being too fearful to react to life because of the adversity we may face, it is time that we make things happen.

You are God's creation. He holds every key to your life, and no Doctor or circumstance can change that. We often ask why God does not save us from the storm. Storms are part of our human nature and are from the changing conditions of this world. Jesus did not come to change the weakness of the human nature or the physical conditions of this world, but to change the hearts of men and women. He does not always stop the storms, but He is always present with us in the storms to give us the inner strength to weather the storms!!!

love reading a journal that a precious friend wrote in every time we talked and she wrote down so many intricate details for me.

How could I ever be happy again, find peace, find joy in my life? That is when God took me to Romans 15:13 on Sept. 5, 2004, not even a month after Jeff had passed. It says, "May the God of hope fill you with all joy and peace as you trust in him, so that you may overflow with hope by the power of the Holy Spirit." I was reminded once again, God is the centerpiece and we are his creation; His purpose in us is to convict our hearts and gain our repentance, so we may once again live in his vast mightiness. It may have taken a beast to conquer my husband's turmoil within himself, but he did not lose the battle on Aug. 10, 2004 here on earth, but came out victorious because he now sits at the feet of my sweet Jesus.

"When all our enemies heard about this, all the surrounding nations were afraid and lost their self-confidence, because they realized that this work had been done with the help of our God." Nehemiah 6:16 (NIV)

"This day is holy to the Lord your God. Do not mourn or weep." For all the people had been weeping as they listened to the words of the Law. "Nehemiah said, "Go and enjoy choice food and sweet drinks, and send some to those who have nothing prepared. This day is holy to our Lord. Do not grieve, for the joy of the Lord is your strength." Nehemiah 8:9-10

Peace and joy became the gifts that my Father gave me as my daily bread. I was reminded by scripture that I was to worship Him for who He is and how He has so greatly blessed me. With a true heart of worship and gratitude, I was able to find joy even in the midst of the rough waters surrounding my family. His glory brightens the world around us. He will bring good to those who love Him.

God continues to use others to pray and lift up my family, but I know a closer more intimate friendship with God has truly carried me all the way.

challenges that lay ahead of us nor the joy Blake would bring to so many people.

Blake was always unique and different from other children. He never played appropriately with toys or cared anything about playing with other children. He spoke and then lost all language only to speak again in third person. At the age of two he was quoting books verbatim. He had an incredible memory for anything I read him or he saw on TV. He memorized the children's catechism as though he was learning his colors. He could quote scripture I taught him at length, but could not do simple things that other toddlers could do. Having taught at a school for disabled children I recognized the characteristics of autism when he was about 18 months old. My conclusions were confirmed when he was four years old.

Throughout our early years of Blake's life, we never wavered from the truth that God would never give us more than we could handle. He showed us glimpses of Blake's understanding of the supremacy of God with his innocent affirmations that "God would always take care of him" when we warned him of stranger danger, or his quoting the Ten Commandments to us, by the number; if we even thought about "fudging the truth." Once Randy tried to get him to tell me a white lie as a joke and Blake replied, " I do not know whether to break commandment number five or nine..." Blake has taught us the importance of remembering the Sabbath. Once as we were having church friends over on a Saturday night and Blake came in the den at 8:00 and said, " I hope you have enjoyed your evening, but it is time for you to go. We have to prepare our hearts for worship." He was five at the time.

When we became pregnant with our second child, Blake was nine and said, "I hope that he or she is obedient." When we asked him why he would say that, he said, "If everyone obeyed the laws of the Lord and the laws of our land, imagine how our lives would be."

He never takes one bite of a snack or meal without first praying thanks to God. He prays fervently and consistently when someone gives him a prayer request. Since the day we told him we were having a baby girl he has prayed for Parker's future husband. He prays that his parents are raising him to walk in the ways of the Lord. I know that he has prayed this prayer everyday of her 15 years of life.

Roller Coaster Ride

Robin Howell

Roller coasters take us to the top of the hill and drop us to the lowest dip in a split second.

You squeal with joy or you gasp for breath. You jump right on or you hesitate because you aren't sure what is ahead.

Singleness is often the same. Delighting in your Savior as a single can certainly take you to the highest summit. However, those days come when once again you have to make a decision by yourself and are so overwhelmed that you almost can't breathe.

The holidays from Thanksgiving to Valentine's Day were the hardest for me. Christmas Eve 2008 had me sitting beside the Christmas tree in my house alone once again. It was quiet and beautiful, but I was lonely. The Lord took me to this precious verse from Zephaniah 3:17 which says: "The Lord your God is with you, he is mighty to save. He will take great delight in you, he will quiet you with his love, he will rejoice over you with singing." My Savior who died for me was singing over me and taking delight in me!!!

I rode the roller coaster of singleness for 45 years. There were many days of gasping, but I tried to look for joy in the journey. I spent time with family, friends, children, and traveled the world to smooth the ride. Investing time with my Savior helped me to see that my devotion as a single was to Him and Him alone. He was my partner for the ride. He held me tightly when the curves slung me where I didn't want to go. He was my eyes when I couldn't see what was ahead. He wept with me when the tears flowed like a river. He danced with me when I wanted to rejoice!

Singleness has twists and turns, but our Lord and Savior will be your forever partner and never leave you on the ride alone!!

Visit Robin's Facebook Page for her book, "I Remember"
www.facebook.com/irememberbook

cold. I just wept and began to let Him know how thankful I was that He had saved me. That's it!

Finally, my faith was put in this tangible world through a true understanding of Christ's suffering for me. I knew that He was going to be with me every step of the way. I had the peace of His forgiveness and His presence to move forward as a single parent, with single-mindedness, that I'd never known before. He became the "Father to the fatherless" and the "Husband to the husbandless." He directed my steps to finish my bachelor degree and pursue a master's degree. This was all to get me to the place where He wanted me to be, so that I'd meet the "man of my dreams," that is the man HE had for me!!

As I share this, we're celebrating our 18th Anniversary. It's God's success story, which I feel compelled to share. "Blessed are those who have learned to acclaim You, who walk in the light of Your presence, O Lord." Psalm 89:15

24, but I remember the tender joy that came the day I said, "You don't have to explain it to me. I will trust you anyway."

That's the kind of joy the world does not understand. That's the kind of joy it can't take away.

Jane blogs at www.janebateman.com
Conference speaker and author of "I WILL NEVER"

ear anymore and I still need time for quiet after being in the mall, grocery store, or any place loud and crowded.

Has this loss kept me down or stolen my joy? Not at all. When God takes something away (like some of my hearing) He gives us something greater (like a clearer awareness of others around us). I feel like for the first time I am not only listening to others, but I am hearing them too. The same goes for the Lord, He has spoken volumes to me this past year. I am praising Him today and always for His joy.

I have this verse printed and hanging on my bathroom wall; 1 Thessalonians 5:16-18 "Be joyful always; pray continually; give thanks in all circumstances, for this is God's will for you in Christ Jesus." In the midst of my loss, I chose joy.

Blogger at www.theneal-family.blogspot.com

email: susanbneal@gmail.com

dad. God laughed when I doubted Him and simply said, "watch this, daughter."

I found joy in Christ again; I started worshiping in church and really taking in the meaning of the words. I started to enjoy being a Christian again. The fire that was once burning in my soul was reignited. Through all the tears and the sleepless nights, I learned that God never gives us more than we can handle. We have the strength in Him to persevere. I have been broken, but that is what needed to happen. God needed me broken so that I could depend on Him to fix me, shape me, and mold me into His perfect daughter. I have a God who had never let me down. My hope comes from Him alone.

The verse that has helped me the most is Job 1:21, "For the Lord has given me what I had and the Lord has taken it away, praise the name of the Lord." God showed me how strong He is. He took me from the lowest point in my life and brought me to this exact spot. I am who I am because of who He is.

When Hubs had his last birthday, I set out a breakfast bowl, orange juice glass and a box of Cocoa Krispies for my birthday guy. I taped the same crumpled plastic "Happy Birthday" banner that we have used at every family birthday for the last 25 years, on the bathroom mirror with I LOVE YOU written in lipstick. I could imagine his smile when he stumbled into the bathroom barely awake and was greeted with a crazy moment just for him.

Joy & celebration. No matter he has told me no gifts and "I am all he needs." This makes me smile, of course, because those words are what my parents would say to each other. It's true though-stuff is stuff and while it is great to be given more stuff on special days, each other, day after day is truly all that matters.

I will embrace this one life I have-with the mess and hardness, celebrations and joy-it is what happened and keeps happening while we are busy making other plans-and for this one life I am incredibly grateful.

Nancy Bouwens - Writer & Coach

Simply Abundant Life Coaching
Live your Life on Purpose for a Purpose!

www.simplyabundantlife.com
www.facebook.com/simplyabundantlifecoaching

However, even though I experienced frustration along the way, I did not allow my circumstances to discourage me. I ended up purchasing the house, beating all odds and closed on the house on April 20th-10 days before I had to be out of my rental after everyone including the lender, told me I wouldn't close before the 30th. Thank God, I didn't become discouraged and give up. I now have a home with a big chunk of equity should I choose to sell, when many others are still upside down on mortgages. It was a blessing in disguise! In the battle, I maintained my peace and kept my trust in God that He would do the impossible and He did!

Stacie L. Buck, author of e-Book, "Transformed, 30 Day Devotional" Coach, President & Founder Diamond Shapers International, LLC , Stacie blogs at www.diamondshapers.com

You can contact Stacie at:

Email: stacie@diamondshapers.com
Facebook: www.facebook.com/diamondstacie
Twitter: twitter.com/DiamondStacie

two hours' drive from where we lived. Since we weren't fluent in Spanish, our good friend Hector accompanied us as our translator.

Upon arriving, Pastor Lalo informed us that their village had been without running water for nearly a month due to a shortage or some other problem they were experiencing. To be honest, I can't recall the exact reason. As a result, villagers were forced to walk to a nearby lake where they filled buckets and large plastic barrels.

How would you and I respond to being without running water for a month, let alone a day?

Over the course of our three days with Pastor Lalo and his congregation, Shelley and I witnessed a depth of joy and generosity that we've rarely seen since. Day after day, people would shower us with gifts, hospitality and amazing food. Men and women alike practically broke their backs to ensure we had enough water for our needs. If ever there was a vivid example of the lyrics in the song above being lived out, it was in these precious brothers and sisters.

Pastor Lalo had a smile that radiated the joy of the Lord flowing from the depths of his soul. This was a man who lived on the meager weekly offerings of his congregation. And yet, when it was time to depart Caoba, this humble man of God insisted on blessing us with the funds collected from all three nightly church services.

Finally, the Lord allowed us to witness one last miracle before our departure...

Running water returned to the village!

The church had been praying for nearly a month and we were able to see this breakthrough on our last day there. Talk about overflowing joy! You would have thought we all won the lottery.

As we left this impoverished little village with tears in our eyes, we realized we had witnessed a clear glimpse of the Kingdom of God. This was true joy that rises above circumstances.

It was a refreshing taste of Living Water.

CJ is an author and speaker and can be contacted at
www.christianspeakers.tv
cj@cjhitz.com

His most recent book is "21 Stories of Generosity"

Tammy blogs at: http://tammyidobelieve.wordpress.com/
You can contact her at: tammyidobelieve@gmail.com
Author of "I Do Believe; Help Me With my Unbelief!"

Nevertheless, God has sustained us. He listens to us literally cry out to Him. He enables me to still sing for the joy that is within me (and hasn't left me) in choir every Sunday. I still teach His Word fervently in Bible Fellowship. Why? Because He said, He would never leave us nor forsake us. He has drawn us closer and closer to Him and each other through all this. Yes, we could have blamed Him and we surely did question and doubt sometimes. But, He has given us the hope in Jesus Christ that keeps us going - even when we don't feel like going. We have found His promise to be true. His Mercies and Grace are truly new with each new dawn we face.

We have learned so very much on our journey lately; about ourselves, about each other, about our marriage and especially about our wonderful loving God.

And we have learned the power of prayer! Multiples of people in our church and around the world are praying for us!! I see the love and compassion of God in their eyes as they ask how we are doing. I have learned about staying in God's Word and in fellowship with His people, how it strengthens us so! In addition, God is showing us through this that other people around us desperately need prayer too. In praying for them we find peace in our situations. He has taught us that we are not to be the ones in control - He is!

I am constantly in awe and amazed how much He loves us!! In all our weakness and frailties and in our inability to understand, He still gathers us in His arms and reassures us of His love.

This journey is not over - not by a long shot! With Jesus as our front guard and rear guard, we will keep moving forward in His Grace.

He Is Able

Bert Sanders

My parents planned to have two children, a girl and boy; then I came along. I was not planned and I never felt wanted or welcomed in our home.

At approximately seven years of age, I began noticing that I was treated different than my sister and brother. I was bullied all the time, not by strangers, but by my brother and my own dad.

My father's mother, my grandmother, was a Christian and loved Jesus. She lived with us. She was blind from cataracts and could not read her Bible. I started reading the Bible to her when I was eight. She always asked me to read John 3:16, first. Then I would read other scriptures as well to her. My grandmother taught me about God and Jesus during those times we were together.

We did this together for eight years until she passed away. I was sixteen. They were the best years of my life when I was young. When I was nineteen, my father had a stroke - the beating and cursing stopped! I felt a sense of relief after they had stopped. He died when I was 23 years old.

When I started seriously thinking about marriage, I asked God to lead me to a woman who was a Christian, who knew and loved Him. He answered my prayer. He blessed me with a Christian wife and she led me to my Savior Jesus Christ when I was 36. This was the best decision in my life. The Lord blessed us with two precious daughters.

In February 2004, I was on my way to work and had a massive heart attack. The doctor thought my life would be over soon, but God had other plans. During this time, the Lord's presence was in my hospital room, to give me comfort. I was at total peace. Also during this time, I could not pray for healing for myself – I felt God had already done so much for me and He had let me live to sixty, that I couldn't ask for anything else. I was not thinking about anything in this world, I just longed and waited to be with Jesus.

After five weeks, I was discharged from the hospital with congestive heart failure and the cardiologist made an appointment with the heart transplant team at the Medical University of South

family. My joy comes from knowing He has adopted me into His family.

> "Praise be to the God and Father of our Lord Jesus Christ, who has blessed us in the heavenly realms with every spiritual blessing in Christ. For he chose us in him before the creation of the world to be holy and blameless in his sight. In love he predestined us for adoption to sonship through Jesus Christ, in accordance with his pleasure and will— to the praise of his glorious grace, which he has freely given us in the One he loves. In him we have redemption through his blood, the forgiveness of sins, in accordance with the riches of God's grace that he lavished on us. With all wisdom and understanding, he made known to us the mystery of his will according to his good pleasure, which he purposed in Christ, to be put into effect when the times reach their fulfilment—to bring unity to all things in heaven and on earth under Christ. In him we were also chosen, having been predestined according to the plan of him who works out everything in conformity with the purpose of his will,…" Ephesians 1:3-11

I am so excited to have my Heavenly Father watching over me. All He has done for me is priceless; there are just no words to express how much I love Him.

Jesus, I love you.

anything about it at the moment I filled in the estimate for the monthly contract of $375 for twelve months. I had never heard of this company nor prospected them; they were simply on my answering machine when I returned from my trip. As I pulled away, I suddenly realized what the Lord had done. I was blown away. He had just proven Himself to me.

This same type of incident became a regular occurrence. Sure, I had hard times with customers complaining and dropping me. Sometimes I had as many as ten or fifteen customers drop me all at once. Panic would always seem to be my default. "What was I going to do?" I'd ask myself as my heart raced. At those times, and to this day, I push myself to remember all the times that the Lord has been there and has provided for me. One day, I was doing one of the yards with my crew and my cell phone rang. It was a man named Michael Collins with BMW Manufacturing. I had heard that they had come to town, but I was just a small time young man with a lawn service. I was shocked. Why was he calling me? We made an appointment and a week later, I was at the top of the Montgomery Building in downtown Spartanburg signing papers. The employees of BMW had to figure out how to even hire a contractor, as I was BMW's very first contractor hired when they came to town.

Years later, married with two children, I'm in full-time Christian ministry, helping men and women affected by homosexuality and seeking freedom. I started Truth Ministry, now Hope for Wholeness National Network, back in 1999, while I still had Carolina Green. I had many plates spinning, but I was being faithful to whatever the Lord was putting on my plate. People asked me, "Do you ever see yourself being full-time in ministry?" I would always respond, "If the Lord lays it on my wife's heart." Five years after starting the ministry, my wife turned to me in our office and said, "I believe it's time for us to sell Carolina Green and be full-time in ministry." When I sold Carolina Green, the fifteen-year contract with BMW MC, that was 30% of our gross revenue, was sold as a portion of the company's assets.

Certainly there have been times over the years in ministry where I had no idea how bills would be paid. Still today, it's paycheck to paycheck. I used to allow so much anxiety to come on me over money. I've learned that it's COMPLETELY USELESS. In the hard times

Trophy of Grace

Pat Freeman

"Because Your love is better than life, my lips will glorify You. I will praise You as long as I live." Psalm 63:3-4

I want to be a testimony to the power of God's healing and deliverance in a time of loss. If we live long enough we will all at some time in our life experience a loss. It may be the loss of a child, parent, sibling, a close friend, a spouse or maybe the loss of a job or financial stability.

I want to be a trophy of grace, God's grace.

I grew up in a Christian home. I do not remember a time when I did not love Jesus. I was in church on Sunday morning, evening, and Wednesday evenings. When I was ten, I made a public profession of faith and was baptized. I went to a Christian University and married my high school sweetheart. Four years later my husband felt that God was calling him into the ministry. We had a great marriage and a great life. Then my husband made some bad choices and left our marriage of 29 years. My world as I knew it came crashing down. I fought for my marriage for over a year, but my husband continued to spiral downward. Never did I think that I would be divorced. Ministers don't leave their wives.

I had very few friends who walked with me through this hard time in my life. I walked around in a stupor and could not even think coherently. It was only by God's grace that I could function on my job. One of my friends was a counselor and told me, "Pat, your boys feel as if they have lost their dad, and now they really need their mom. You need to eat, sleep and exercise." My eating consisted of just a protein bar; my sleep came after I would immerse myself in Psalms; and my exercise was a long walk very early in the morning. On many of those walks I would just pour out my heart to God and then I would sing praise songs to Him.

I moved to a new town, started a new life with a new job, new church, new home, and new friends.

True Joy Through the Grief

Joanie Martin

I have realized in the past 2 years that without hope you cannot have joy...especially when life seems to be spiraling out of control. My precious mother struggled with clinical depression for 35 years and many suicide attempts before the Lord decided it was enough and allowed her to come home. Her mind was clouded by hopelessness and she lost her joy.

My sister, who is my closest friend, was diagnosed with an auto-immune disorder and lymphoma a few months later. I thought this would be my challenge for 2013 because surely my family had been through enough. But, I was wrong.

In April of the same year, my husband and I got an early morning phone call from a coroner in Charleston, SC. My beloved 29-year-old son, the one who left what seemed to be a promising career to go back to school to follow a dream, had taken his life. There were no signs that he was struggling. I miss him desperately.

What do you do with all this if you have no hope? By hope, I mean the hope that only comes in knowing and trusting without a doubt that God is who He says He is...Redeemer, Savior, my Anchor, my Hope. Knowing His Word is to be trusted when He says if you, "confess with your mouth that Jesus is Lord, and believe in your heart that God raised him from the dead, then you will be saved." Romans 10:9

My mother, my sister, and my son knew and know Him as their own Savior and Lord. Trusting that, I have hope...to know that this life lasts only a moment compared to eternity and my hope comes in believing that one day I will see Jesus face to face. I will then see all my loved ones once again. This is my hope. This hope in Jesus and His promises is what gives me joy this side of eternity!

Psalm 126:5-6 says, "those who sow with tears will reap with songs of joy. Those who go out weeping, carrying seed to sow, will return with songs of joy, carrying sheaves with them."

I have decided that I don't want any of these trials to be for nothing. I don't want to just weep, but seek to continue finding ways

A Choice to Make

Dwayne Morris

If you could travel anywhere in the world, where would you go? Paris? Hawaii? Australia? That's a fun question to consider when you are pretty sure it will never happen, but everything changes when you find out that you can actually pick a destination of your choice. You begin thinking about the trip and the experience of actually being in a place you've only heard about in the past. Before long, you begin eagerly awaiting your trip.

I believe this was the Apostle Paul's experience about going to visit the band of Christians in Rome. He longed to be with them so much that he shared, "...without ceasing I make mention of you always in my prayers, making request if, by some means, now at last I may find a way in the will of God to come to you." (Romans 1:9) It is clear that Paul had a strong desire to visit his Christian brothers and sisters. In fact, a little later in verse 13, we read he made plans to get there, but was hindered. And yet, Paul never stopped praying for the opportunity to go visit the Christians in Rome (his words).

Here's the kicker: Paul never allowed his circumstances to steal his joy. In fact, later he declared a phrase that many a Christian has uttered in times of uncertain outcome, "The just shall live by faith." (Romans 1:17) That's a lot easier to say than to live. It sure is easy to say that when you're the one trying to encourage, not so much when you're the one trying to keep your world from falling apart.

That's the real test. When we are face to face with challenging circumstances, and we have a choice to make with our reactions: Do we panic and see no further than the obstacle in front of us; or do we pause long enough to realize that God really is in control, and whatever has birthed fear and uncertainty in our lives is part of what He's doing for our good?

Zac Smith was faced with such a scenario. Diagnosed with Stage Four Colon Cancer, he had a choice to make about the obstacle in his life.

Zac Smith was a healthy thirty-two year old with a beautiful wife, three children, a home, and a job he loved. Diagnosed with Stage Four

This is the amazing part of Zac's story. His perspective on his obstacle did not open up bouts of anger and bitterness. Rather it positioned him to welcome cancer as a vehicle for God to be glorified. His strongest statement about his battle with cancer says it best:

"If God chooses to heal me, God is God and God is good. If God chooses not to heal me and allows me to die, God is God and God is still good. To God be the glory."

Zac won his battle with cancer by stepping out of his body here on Earth into the presence of the One who created his body and the cancer that took his life. Zac saw his joy and hope fulfilled both here on Earth and in Heaven. And because of his faithfulness, his name and his faith lives today as people share about the peace and joy he experienced that many will never experience because they live by their own strength and experience the emptiness outside of Jesus Christ.

Dwayne Morris, Blogger, Speaker and author of "the Outrageous life,"

Keep up with Dwayne:

blog: www.morrismatters.com
Twitter: @DwayneMorris
Facebook: www.facebook.com/dwaynemorris

And be aware of our enemy's ploy
Your love, the hope of our world, the freedom for every heart
This is my joy that fuels my life and my art
This joy that is not only attainable but accessible
To walk in, to breathe in, to live out your parable

You can connect with Denica at:
http://denicalynn.blogspot.com/
https://www.facebook.com/#!/denicamccallwriter

Week One   Introduction

Before class, you will need to download and print enough sheets for your class. You can find the download at www.askgodtoday.com under "Free Downloads," PDF titled: Joy Zappers

1. Welcome everyone to class.

2. Pass around a signup sheet requesting names, addresses, emails and cell phone numbers for contact info. Please pray for each of these people during the five weeks of study. Also, try to make some sort of contact with them throughout the five weeks to encourage them. Try to check on them if they miss a week. People need to know you care and miss them when they are absent.

3. I suggest you do an Icebreaker to help people get to know each other better and help them laugh and enjoy the time together. Here is one I did, but you can come up with your own if you wish:

   Desert Island

   Items needed: Blank sheets of paper (index card size), Pen or pencil

   Announce, 'You've been exiled to a deserted island for a year. In addition to the essentials, you may take one piece of music, one book (which is not a Bible) and one luxury item you can carry with you (i.e.not a boat to leave the island!) What would you take and why?

   Allow a few minutes for the people to draw up their list of three items, before sharing their choices with the rest of the group. Make sure everyone shares their name as well.   As with most icebreakers and relationship building activities, it's good for the group leaders to join in too!

4. Watch the video – approximately 20 minutes.

Parents
Job
Stress
Thoughts
Negativity
Addictions
Pain
Sin
Challenges
School
Disappointments
Insecurities
Grief
Fear
Other

We all have life issues that can zap the joy right out of us. The question is, "How long are you going to let those issues control your joy?"

Top 5 that you have trouble with:

1.
2.
3.
4.
5.

Now, which is the #1 Joy Zapper in your life? Be specific.

Week Two   Joy Down in My Heart Discussion

Before class, you will need to download and print enough sheets for your class. You can find the download at www.askgodtoday.com under "Free Downloads," PDF titled: Honor God For His Holiness

Answers for "Honor God For His Holiness"

Honor God for His Holiness - Answers

How can we honor God?
1. Recognizing His Holiness – He is sovereign, He is all-knowing, all-powerful, omnipresent (He is everywhere).
2. By confessing and repenting of all our sinful thoughts, words, and deeds.
3. By volunteering to serve Him and others.
4. By persevering in difficult and demanding circumstances.
5. By accepting the tasks to which He has called us.
6. By trusting Him and having faith in Him.
7. By glorifying His name.

I Want to be Like Jesus!! Who Is He?

Jesus was God in the flesh and full of grace and truth. John 1:14
Jesus is the image of the invisible God. Col 1:15
Jesus is the son of God. John 3:17
Jesus is before all things, and in Him all things hold together. Col 1:17
Jesus is the head over every power and authority. And in Him you have been given fullness. Col 2:9-10
Jesus is our Redeemer. John 3:16
Jesus forgives you all your sins…nailing them to the cross. Col 2:13
Jesus is the Way, the Truth, and the Life. John 14:6
Jesus is the Light of the world. John 8:12
Jesus loves you and He commands us to love one another just as He loved you. John 15:12
Jesus laid down His life for you. John 15:13
Jesus overcame temptations. Matt 4:1-11
Jesus was a giver. Matt 14:16
Jesus was a teacher, preacher, and healer. Matt 4:23
Jesus is gentle and humble and in Him you will find rest. Matt 11:29
Jesus prayed and believed. Matt 26:36
Jesus was obedient. Matt 26:39
Jesus gives strength and in Him you can do ALL things. Phil 4:13
Jesus had JOY and it may be made complete in you. John 15:12
Jesus gives wisdom and knowledge. Col 2:2-3

6. Day Nine – Application #1 – Does anyone want to share their answer? Offer to pray for them.

7. Day Ten – Discuss the power of prayer.

8. Day Eleven – Application #4 – Does anyone want to share their answer here and how they handled it?

9. Day Twelve – Read Isaiah 41:8-10 Encourage your group by explaining God tells us not to fear and He will uphold us and always be with us.

10. Day Thirteen – Discuss Matthew 6:33. What is God promising us here and what is our part in this?

11. Day Fourteen – Ask Application #2 question and open for discussion.

12. As the leader, it is your choice whether you want to take prayer requests.

13. Close in prayer.

Week Four   Don't Give Up Discussion

Before class, you will need to download and print enough sheets for your class. You can find the download at www.askgodtoday.com under "Free Downloads," PDF titled: "Begin with the End in Mind…" by Dwayne Morris.

1. Welcome everyone to class.

2. Play the Joy Beyond video – approximately 20 minutes.

3. Hand out the sheet "Begin with the End in Mind…"

10. Day Twenty – Ask: Does everyone know what it means to detach? What are some ways that you detach from a situation? Does it help? What happens if you don't detach yourself?

11. Day Twenty-one – Ask: Has there ever been anything in your past that you didn't make it through? Remind everyone – that no matter what the situation, God will help you make it through. We ALWAYS make it through. This too shall pass!

12. As the leader, it is your choice whether you want to take prayer requests.

13. Close in prayer.

Week Five   No Matter What Discussion

1. Welcome everyone to class.

2. Play the Joy Beyond video – approximately 20 minutes.

3. Start the facilitation of the discussion. Open with prayer. Circle up and lead them through each day, asking if there is anything they read this week that made an impact on them. Ask if they would be willing to share.

4. Day Twenty-two – Ask: Do you really think it is better to give than receive? Why? Brenda named a few things that we can give away – smiles, love, joy, hugs, kind words, laughter, time, grace, mercy, forgiveness, resources, and so much more. Ask: Does anyone have a story from their own life they can share where they were either blessed by someone or tried to be a blessing to someone?

5. Day Twenty-three – Ask: Can anyone share the last time they had a pity party? Go over Application: #1, #2, #3, and #4.

6. Day Twenty-four – Ask: Can anyone tell you what it means to persevere? Ask: Why do you think God wants us to persevere?

Week Six   Stories From the Heart

Before class, ask if anyone would be willing to share a short testimony of how they discovered joy through Christ or how this book has helped them. Please bring blank paper to hand out for testimonies to be written on. Also, please go to the Free Downloads on www.askgodtoday<http://www.askgodtoday/> and print copies of the "Joy Beyond Testimonial Questions."

1. Welcome everyone to class.

2. Play the Joy Beyond Video.

3. Ask if anyone can share something that may have impacted them out of all the stories from the contributors in the book.

4. Have paper available and hand a piece out to everyone and ask them to take a few minutes to write their own story of a time in their life when they discovered joy through Christ beyond the circumstances of their own life.

5. Tell them if they want, to please email them to **brendamcgraw@yahoo.com** or fax to Brenda at 864-578-2755.

6. Hand out the "Joy Beyond Testimonial Questions." Have everyone take about 5 to 10 minutes to complete and then hand back into you. After the class is over, please either email this to **brendamcgraw@yahoo.com** or fax to 864-578-2755. This will go directly to Brenda McGraw to help make any improvements and to know how I can better serve and pray for everyone. Please indicate your name as the leader of the class when sending these to me.

End Notes - Resources by Brenda McGraw

Foreword - Genesis 2:24, 1 Corinthians 7:15, Psalm 84

Introduction - Psalm 126:2-6, Psalm 92:4-5, Psalm 89:1-2

Week One - Joy Down in My Heart - Psalm 92:4-5, Psalm 89:1-2

Day 1 - 1 Thessalonians 5:16-18
Day 2 - Romans 12:2, 2 Corinthians 10:5, Romans 8:6, Philippians 4:8-9
Day 3 - Acts 20:35, Philippians 2:2-7, Romans 8:5-8, Luke 6:38,
    Philippians 4:5
Day 4 - 1 Thessalonians 5:21-22
Day 5 - Psalm 90:14, Psalm 13:5, Psalm 57:7, 10, Psalm 63:1, 3-5b,
    Psalm 33:22, Psalm 107:9, Psalm 145:16, 17, 19
Day 6 - Isaiah 55:8-9, James 1:22, James 1:5, 6, 8
Day 7 - Philippians 4:4, Psalm 4:7, 1 Peter 1:8, "I've Got the Joy In My
    Heart," Salvation: Romans 3:10,23, Romans 10:13, John 3:16,
    John 1:12, Romans 10:9

Week Two - The God of Hope

Day 8 - Psalm 67:1, Proverbs 3:3-4, Numbers 6:24-26
Day 9 - Romans 8:31, Romans 8:31-35, 37, Psalm 34:4, Hebrews 11:1,
    Philippians 4:6, Psalm 16:11, 2 Timothy 1:7
Day 10- James 5:13-18
Day 11- Romans 15:13, Romans 5:1-5, 2 Corinthians 5:17,
    James 4:14-15
Day 12- Isaiah 41:10
Day13- Deuteronomy 4:24, Matthew 6:33, Matthew 6:25-34,
    Psalm 73:26
Day14- Psalm 28:2, Psalm 28:7
    Songs suggested: "Hold On," Jamie Grace; "Stronger," Mandisa;
    "Good Morning," Mandisa; "Get Back Up," Toby Mac; "So Long
    Self," Mercy Me; "Overcomer," Mandisa